Friedrich Schiller, Captain Blaquiere

The History of the Thirty Years War in Germany

Vol. II

Friedrich Schiller, Captain Blaquiere

The History of the Thirty Years War in Germany
Vol. II

ISBN/EAN: 9783337014308

Printed in Europe, USA, Canada, Australia, Japan

Cover: Foto ©ninafisch / pixelio.de

More available books at **www.hansebooks.com**

THE
HISTORY
OF THE
THIRTY YEARS WAR
IN
GERMANY.

TRANSLATED FROM THE ORIGINAL GERMAN

OF

FREDERIC SCHILLER,

AULIC COUNSELLOR, AND PROFESSOR OF PHILOSOPHY
AT JENA,

BY

CAPTAIN BLAQUIERE,
OF THE ROYAL IRISH ARTILLERY.

IN TWO VOLUMES.

VOL. II.

LONDON:
PRINTED FOR W. MILLER, OLD BOND STREET.
1799.

TABLE OF CONTENTS.

VOLUME THE SECOND.

BOOK III.

PROGRESS *of Gustavus Adolphus.—Wirtzburg taken.—The Duke of Lorrain defeated.—Frankfort taken.—Capture of Mentz.—Negotiations of Sweden with Bavaria.—Defeat and Death of Tilly.—Munich taken.—The Saxon Army enters Bohemia, and takes Prague.—Wallenstein reassumes the Command of the Imperial Army.—Gustavus Adolphus defends Nuremberg.—Reinforced.—Attacks Wallenstein's Intrenchments.—Repulsed.—Loss of both Armies.—Gustavus Adolphus enters Saxony.—Battle of Lutzen.—Gustavus Adolphus killed.—Pappenheim mortally wounded.—Reflections.*

Page 1 to 169.

BOOK

BOOK IV.

Closer Alliance between France and Sweden.—Efforts of France.—Congress at Hailbron.—Mutiny of the Swedish Army.—The Duke of Weimar takes Ratisbon.—Wallenstein enters Silesia.—Defeats a Corps of Swedes.—Begins to form dangerous Designs.—Forsaken by his Army.—Retires to Egra.—His Associates assassinated.—Illo's Bravery.—Wallenstein murdered.—His Character. Page 171 to 251.

CONTINUATION.

Battle of Nordlingen.—The Swedes defeated.—Negotiations.—Miseries in Germany.—Treaty of Prague.—Saxony joins Austria.—Victory at Wittstock.—The Duke of Weimar defeated at Rheinfelden.—Returns, and totally defeats the Austrians.—His Death and Character.—Denmark embraces the Emperor's Party.—The Austrian Army destroyed.—Swedish Victory at Iankowitz.—French defeated at Freyburg.—Are victorious at Allensheim.—Ferdinand III.—Peace with the Elector of Bavaria.—Returns to the Alliance of Austria.—Melander killed.—Peace. Page 252 to the end.

HISTORY

OF THE

THIRTY YEARS WAR.

BOOK III.

THE glorious victory of Gustavus Adolphus had effected a great change in the conduct of that monarch, and in the opinion which both his friends and his enemies entertained of him. He had confronted himself with the greatest general of the age, and by the force of his tactics and Swedish valour, conquered the Imperial troops, the best in Europe. From that instant he relied upon himself, and self-reliance has ever been the parent of great actions. Had not Alexander's impetuosity triumphed upon the Granicus, never had that conqueror overturned the Persian empire. Bolder and more dexterous measures were henceforward observed in the operations of the Swedish king; greater resolutions, even under unfavourable circumstances,

stances, more defiance towards his adversaries, greater mildness to his friends, and forbearance towards his enemies. His native courage was also augmented by his piety. He readily confounded his own cause with that of Heaven; and **beheld** in Tilly's defeat the work of Divine vengeance. His crown was **now** risked upon German ground, which had for centuries beheld no foreign enemy. The warlike disposition of **its** inhabitants, the vigilance of its numerous princes, the artful confederacy of its states, **the** multitude of **its** strong castles, **and** the course of its rivers, had hitherto restrained the ambition of its neighbours; and when attacked upon its extensive frontier, it was still secured in its interior. At the most remote periods this Empire maintained the equivocal prerogative of being its own enemy, and of being secured against every foreign force. It was also the want of union among its members, and an intolerant zeal for religion, which now procured the Swedish conqueror an entrance into its territories. The bond of harmony was already dissolved, which had rendered this Empire hitherto invincible; and it was from Germany itself that Gustavus Adolphus acquired the power of subjecting it. With prudence equal to his courage, he seized the favourable moment;

ment; and equally expert in the cabinet as in the field, he employed the resources of a consummate policy with as much effect as the thunder of his cannon. Uninterrupted, he pursued his victory in Germany, without once losing sight of his own dominions.

The consternation of the Emperor, and of the Catholic League, could not exceed the astonishment of the Swedish allies at the King's unexpected good fortune. His exploits surpassed even the most ardent expectations. The formidable army which had checked his progress, set bounds to his ambition, and rendered him dependant upon his friends, was now annihilated. Single, and without a competitor, he appeared in the midst of Germany; nothing could stop his career, or interrupt his pretensions, were he, even in the intoxication of success, inclined to abuse his victory. If the Emperor's authority was formidable in the commencement, equal fears might now be entertained, from the impetuosity of a foreign conqueror, for the constitution of the Empire, and, from the zeal of a Protestant king, for the Catholic church of Germany. The distrust and jealousy which had for some time subsided in the minds of several of the combined powers towards the Emperor was now rekindled, and scarcely had Gustavus Adolphus merited their confidence, when they began to oppose obstacles to his designs. He was obliged to purchase his victories amid a continual struggle with the artifice of his enemies and the jealousy of confederates: but his resolute courage and deep penetration overcame every obstruction. While, by the success of his arms, he excited the attention of his more powerful allies, France and Saxony, he raised the courage of the weaker states, and drew from them an open declaration of their sentiments. Those who fought in the same cause with Gustavus Adolphus formed greater expectations from the magnanimity of this great ally, who enriched them with the spoils of their enemies, protected them against oppression; and, inconsiderable in themselves, they acquired a weight when united with the Swedish hero. This was the case with most of the free cities, and, above all, with the inferior Protestant states. It was by these means that the King was introduced into the heart of Germany, his rear was covered, his army was provided with necessaries, his troops were received into their fortresses, and their lives exposed in his battles. His prudent respect for the national pride, his amiable deportment,

ment, some brilliant acts of justice, and his regard for the laws, were so many fetters with which he attached to him the German Protestants; while the revolting barbarities of the Imperialists, the Spaniards, and troops of Lorrain, powerfully contributed to place the forbearance of his own army in a favourable light.

If Gustavus Adolphus owed most of his progress to his own genius, it must not be denied that he was greatly favoured by the nature of circumstances and his good fortune. He had two great advantages upon his side, which gained him a decided superiority over his enemies. While he removed the theatre of the war to the territories of the League, joined to his army the recruits of those countries, enriched them with plunder, and appropriated to himself the revenues of such princes as had fled, he was enabled to prevent an effectual resistance upon the part of his enemies, and maintain an expensive war with little cost to himself. When, moreover, his opponents, the princes of the League, were divided among themselves, and acted without union, consequently without effect; when generals wanted authority, their troops obedience, and their scattered armies had no mutual dependance; while the leaders of

of the forces were in opposition to the statesman and the minister, both were united in
Gustavus Adolphus, from whom all authority
came, and upon whom the soldiers' eyes were
turned. He was alone the soul of his party,
the author of his plans, and the executor
of them. By his means all the affairs of the
Protestants acquired an union and harmony
which was wanting altogether among their
enemies. It was not then surprising, if, favoured
by such advantages, at the head of such an
army, endowed with such a genius and such
consummate policy, Gustavus Adolphus was
irresistible.

With the sword in one hand, and mercy
in the other, he now traversed the German
territories, as conqueror and legislator, with
as much rapidity as he could have done
upon a tour of pleasure; the keys of every
fortress are delivered to him as readily as
to the native sovereign; no castle is longer
inaccessible, no river stops his progress, and
he often vanquished by the terror of his name.
His standards are now seen flying along
the Maine, the Lower Palatinate is delivered,
and the Spaniards and the troops of Lorrain
have fled over the Rhine and the Moselle.
The

The Swedes and Hessians now entered with
impetuosity the territories of Mentz, Bamberg,
and Wirtzburg; and three fugitive bishops, at
a distance from their sees, dearly suffered for
their unfortunate attachment to the Emperor.
The most culpable of all the princes, Maximilian the chief of the League, at length experienced, upon his own territories, the miseries
which he had prepared for others. Neither the
terrifying prospect of his allies, nor the friendly
overtures of Gustavus, who, amid the career
of his successes, made the most advantageous
offers of peace, could overcome the obstinacy
of this prince, even after the ruin of Tilly,
who had hitherto protected that country as a
guardian angel. Not only the banks of the
Rhine, but those of the Lech and the Danube,
now swarmed with Swedish warriors; retired
into his strong castles, the defeated Elector
abandoned to the enemy his defenceless states
which had hitherto felt no foe, and where the
violences practised by the Bavarians seemed to
invite retaliation. Munich itself opened its
gates to the invincible monarch; and the unfortunate Elector Palatine was enabled, for some
short period, in the forsaken residence of his
adversary, to console himself for the loss of his
kingdom.

At

At the same time that Gustavus Adolphus extended his conquests in the south of Germany, his allies and generals acquired similar triumphs in the other provinces. While he drove the enemy before him, Lower Saxony shook off the Austrian yoke, Mecklenburg was abandoned, and on the borders of the Elbe and Weser the Austrians evacuated all their garrisons. The Landgrave William of Hesse Cassel rendered himself formidable in Westphalia, the Duke of Weimar in Thuringia, and the French in the electorate of Treves. On the eastward the whole kingdom of Bohemia was overrun by the Saxons; the Turks were already prepared to fall upon Hungary; and a dangerous insurrection was meditated in the heart of the Austrian territories. Inconsolable, did the Emperor look around, in expectation of receiving from the different courts of Europe the means of opposing the enemy; in vain did he call to his assistance the Spaniards, whom the bravery of the Flemings occupied within the Rhine; he made efforts equally fruitless to engage in his cause the Court of Rome and the whole Catholic church. The offended Pope sported, by some splendid processions and idle anathemas, with the embarrassment of Ferdinand; and instead

of

of yielding the required affiftance, only fhowed him Mantua laid wafte.

The haughty defpot was now aware of his infignificance; the ruin of his allies, with the departure of his friends, and the continual increafe of danger, fhowed him the vanity of his projects. Surrounded by enemies on every fide of his extenfive dominions; with the countries of the League, the ramparts were gone with which Auftria had hitherto defended herfelf, and the horrors of war approached her unguarded frontiers. His moft zealous confederates were now difarmed, and Maximilian of Bavaria, his firmeft fupport, was fcarce able to defend himfelf; his armies, diminifhed by repeated defeats and defertion, were rendered fpiritlefs, and imbibed a difmay which, by infpiring the terrors of a defeat, already infured a victory over them. The danger had now gained its fummit, and nothing except fome extraordinary means could fave the Houfe of Auftria from deftruction. The moft fenfible want was that of a general, and the only one who was capable of re-eftablifhing the former reputation of the Auftrian arms had been, through jealoufy, removed from the command. So low was the Emperor, however, reduced,

that

that he even made humiliating offers to his offended servant, and proffered to him the power of which he had been shamefully deprived in a still more disgraceful manner. A new spirit now appeared to actuate the decayed body of Austria, and a rapid change of circumstances betrayed the able hand which guided it. To the absolute King of Sweden, a general equally absolute was now opposed, and one victorious hero was confronted with another; both armies renewed the dubious conflict, and the victory, so nearly in the hands of Gustavus Adolphus, must be again exposed to a severe trial. The contending forces encamped before Nuremberg, equally anxious for the event of a battle. The strength of all Germany appeared directed towards this point, and prepared to bring the fate of a twelve years war to a decision. But this cloud was at once dispelled, and forsook Franconia only to hover with a more destructive effect upon the plains of Saxony. Near Lutzen fell the thunder which menaced Nuremberg; and the battle, already half lost, was purchased by the corpse of a sovereign. Fortune, which never hitherto neglected the career of the King of Sweden, favoured him at his death with the rare indulgence of being permitted to die in the full possession of his glory and unrivalled fame.

fame. It may be allowed us to doubt whether, with a longer life, he had merited the tears which Germany shed over his grave, or maintained the tribute which posterity yields the only just conqueror whom this world has produced. By the untimely end of this formidable leader, the ruin of his party was apprehended. But there is no human loss which is irreparable. Two great statesmen, Oxenstern in Germany, and Richelieu in France, undertook the conduct of the war upon the demise of the hero; and destiny still prolonged, for six years, the flames of war which hovered over the ashes of him who was no more.

I may here be permitted to follow Gustavus Adolphus in his victorious progress, and with a rapid view to relate it; and then, when the fortune of the Swedes is reduced to extremity by a series of disasters, and Austria, in the height of its pride, constrained to have recourse to the most desperate and humiliating expedients, to return with the thread of the narration to the Emperor.

The plan of future operations had no sooner been concerted between the King of Sweden and the Elector of Saxony at Halle, in which

it

it was decided that the latter should invade Bohemia, while the former entered the territories of the League; no sooner had an alliance taken place between the princes of Anhalt and Weimar, who prepared to conquer Magdeburg, than the King began his march towards the Empire. The Emperor was still formidable in the Empire; Imperial garrisons still opposed the Swedish progress in Franconia, Suabia, and the Palatinate, most of which must be overcome by force. On the Rhine he was awaited by the Spaniards, who had overrun the territories of the banished Elector Palatine, possessed themselves of all his strong places, and rendered the passage of the river difficult. On his rear was Tilly, who had already begun to assemble new strength; and in a short time that general was to be joined by the auxiliaries of Lorrain. In the bosom of every Papist, religious zeal presented him with an inveterate enemy; and yet his connexions with France did not leave him entirely at liberty to act against the Catholics. Gustavus Adolphus perceived those obstacles, and vanquished them; the strength of the Austrians lay scattered in different garrisons, and he was able to attack them with his united force. If the religious bigotry of the Catholics opposed him,

together

together with the fear in which the weaker
states were retained from apprehensions of Austria, he might rely upon the active support of
the Protestants, alarmed by the thoughts of the
Emperor's tyranny. The ravages of the Imperial and Spanish troops had powerfully aided
him in those quarters; the ill-treated husbandman and citizen had long awaited a deliverer,
and a change of condition appeared a desirable
object to all. Emissaries were already dispatched to gain over the more considerable free
cities, viz. Nuremberg and Frankfort, to the
Swedish side; Erfurt was the first that lay
upon the King's march, and which he could
not leave unoccupied in his rear. A successful
negotiation with the Protestant inhabitants
procured him, without resistance, the entrance
into the city and its citadel. Here, as in all
other places which afterwards submitted to his
arms, he exacted an oath of allegiance, and
he secured its possession by a sufficient garrison.
The command of an army which was destined
to be raised in Thuringia, was given to his ally,
William Duke of Weimar; he also entrusted
his queen to the city of Erfurt, and promised
to increase its privileges. The Swedish army
now broke off in two columns through the
forest of Thuringia, over Gotha; Arnstadt rescued,

cued, during the march, the county of Henneberg from the hands of the Imperialists; and in three days they formed a junction at Koenigshofen, on the borders of Franconia.

Francis, Bishop of Wirtzburg, the most zealous enemy of the Protestants, and the most active member of the Catholic League, was also the first who felt the indignation of Gustavus Adolphus. A few threats were sufficient to obtain the Swedes possession of his fortress of Koenigshofen, and with it the key of the whole territory. Consternation upon this conquest seized all the Catholic states of the Empire; the bishops of Bamberg and Wirtzburg trembled in their residences; they already saw their sees tottering, their churches profaned, and their religion degraded. The animosity and persecuting spirit of his enemies had represented the conduct of the King of Sweden and his troops in the most disadvantageous light, which neither the repeated assurances of the King, nor the most splendid examples of his clemency and patience, could efface; the people feared to suffer the same treatment, which in similar circumstances they would have shown to others. Many of the richest Catholics now fled to avoid the sanguinary fanaticism of the Swedes; the
Bishop

Bishop himself afforded the example to his subjects. In the midst of the persecuting zeal which his bigotry had kindled, he abandoned his dominions, and fled to Paris, in order to endeavour to excite the French ministry against the common enemy of the Catholic religion.

Meanwhile Gustavus Adolphus made a rapid progress amid the ecclesiastical territories. Abandoned by their garrisons, Schweinfurt, and soon after Wirtzburg, surrendered to him; but Marienberg he was obliged to gain by storm. In this place the enemy had collected a great quantity of provisions and warlike necessaries, which now fell into the hands of the Swedes; the King found a valuable prize in the library of the Jesuits, which he transported to Upsal, and his troops a still more agreeable one in the richly filled wine-vaults of the prelate: the Bishop had in seasonable time saved his treasure. The example of the capital was followed by the remainder of the country, and every place submitted to the Swedes. The King caused all the Bishop's subjects to swear him allegiance; and, in the absence of the legitimate sovereign, created a regency, of whom half were composed of Protestants. In every Catholic place of which Gustavus Adolphus made himself the master, he he established the Protestants in all the churches, but without retaliating upon the Papists the oppression which they practised upon the former; force was only used towards such as made resistance; the few violences which the soldiery, amid the blind rage of their first attacks, exercised, cannot be attributed to their humane leader. Such enemies as were peacefully disposed and defenceless, experienced a mild treatment; it was Gustavus Adolphus's most sacred principle to spare the blood of his enemies, as much as that of his own troops. Immediately upon his irruption into the bishopric of Wirtzburg, without regarding the treaties which the Bishop, in order to gain time, had pretended to enter into, he endeavoured to excite the general of the League to assist his country. That defeated commander had in the mean time collected the ruins of his army on the Weser; reinforced himself by the Imperial garrisons in Lower Saxony; and had formed a junction in Hesse Cassel with Fugger and Altringer, who commanded under him. At the head of a considerable force, Tilly burned with ardour to efface the stain of his first defeat by a splendid victory. In the camp of Fulda, where he had led his army, he made use of repeated arguments with the Duke of Bavaria to permit him to give battle to Gustavus Adolphus. But the League had, besides Tilly's, no second army to lose; and Maximilian was too cautious to expose the fortune of his party to the risk of another battle. With tears in his eyes, Tilly received the commands of his superior, which enjoined him to inactivity. In this manner his march towards Franconia was delayed, and Gustavus Adolphus gained time to obtain possession of the whole territory. It was in vain that Tilly reinforced his army near Aschaffenburg with 12,000 troops of Lorrain, in order, with a superior force, to relieve Wirtzburg; both the town and citadel were already in the hands of the Swedes; and Maximilian of Bavaria was universally censured, perhaps not without cause, for having, by his scruples, occasioned the loss of the country. Obliged to avoid a battle, Tilly must now content himself with preventing the further advance of the enemy; but he could only recover a few places from the valour of the Swedes. After an ineffectual attempt to throw a reinforcement of troops into the town of Hanau, which was weakly garrisoned by the Imperialists, and the possession of which was of the utmost importance to the Swedes, he followed

the

the mountain road, to defend the Palatinate
against the approach of the King.

Tilly was not the sole enemy whom Gustavus
Adolphus met in Franconia, and drove before
him. Charles Duke of Lorrain, celebrated in
the cotemporary annals for his unsteadiness of
character, his vain projects, and his misfortunes, ventured to raise his weak arm against
the Swedish hero, in order to obtain from the
Emperor Ferdinand the electoral dignity. Deaf
to the rules of policy, this prince, obeying only
the dictates of his boisterous ambition, exasperated France against him by having recourse to
the Emperor's protection; and exposed in a
strange country, for a vain phantom, his dominions, which a French army overrun. Austria
readily yielded to him the honour, like the
other princes of the League, of hazarding his
ruin for her sake. Intoxicated with vain hopes,
this prince collected a force of 17,000 men,
which he desired to lead in person against
the Swedes. If these troops were deficient
in discipline and bravery, they wanted not
a splendid attire; and however saving they
were of their martial prowess against the enemy,
the more willing they were to display it towards
the people, for whose defence they were arrived.

A panic

A panic terror ftruck them upon the approach of the King's cavalry, and they were eafily expelled from their cantonments in the territories of Wirtzburg; the defeat of a few regiments occafioned an univerfal rout among their troops, and the remainder haftened upon the other fide of the Rhine, to avoid the effect of Swedifh valour. Difgraced and ridiculed throughout all Germany, the Duke returned home, too fortunate in efcaping the indignation of his conqueror, who had firft beaten him in the field, and then juftified his hoftilities by a manifefto. It is related upon this occafion, that a peafant, in a village upon the Rhine, ftruck the Duke's horfe with a whip as he was quickly paffing; " *Hafte, Sir,*" faid the peafant; " *you muft make more fpeed in order* " *to efcape the great King of Sweden.*"

The unfortunate example of his neighbour had infpired the Bifhop of Bamberg with more prudent refolutions. To prevent the plundering of his territories, he fent deputies to the King of Sweden with offers of a peace; but thefe were defigned only to gain time until the arrival of the troops which he expected to his affiftance. Guftavus Adolphus, too magnanimous to fufpect treachery, readily accepted the

the Bishop's offers, and mentioned the conditions upon which he was willing to save the territories of the latter from hostile treatment; he was the more disposed to act in this manner, as he did not wish to lose that time by conquering Bamberg, which he could better employ in prosecuting his designs upon the territories of the Rhine. The rapidity with which he executed those designs obtained him the supplies which the loss of time in pursuing a weak bishop in Franconia must have withheld from him. This cunning prelate neglected the treaty so soon as the danger was removed from his territories; scarce had Gustavus Adolphus departed, when he threw himself under the protection of Tilly, and readily received the Imperial troops into his fortresses, which he had previously offered to the Swedes. By this stratagem, however, he only delayed for a short period the ruin of his bishopric. A Swedish general who had been left in Franconia, undertook to chastise this perfidy; and the country, thus rendered the seat of war, was equally laid waste by friends and enemies.

The flight of the Imperialists, whose formidable presence had hitherto delayed the decision of the Franconian states, had prevented both

both the nobility and peasantry from showing themselves friendly disposed towards the humane conduct of the Swedish king. Nuremberg joyfully received him; and the Franconian nobles were gained by a flattering proclamation, in which the King condescended to justify his hostile entrance into their territories. The fertility of Franconia, and the confidence with which the forbearance of the army inspired its inhabitants, produced abundance in the Swedish camp. The favour into which Gustavus Adolphus insinuated himself among the nobility of this circle, the admiration and regard which his exploits excited, even among his enemies, and the rich booty which the service of a victorious king held out, were not a little serviceable to him. Recruits flocked to his standard from all quarters.

The King had lost little or no time in subduing Franconia. Gustavus Horn, one of his best generals, was left to complete the conquest of this circle, and to preserve it with a force of 8000 men; he hastened himself with the main army, which had been augmented by the recruits of Franconia, towards the Rhine, in order to secure this frontier of the Empire against the Spaniards; to disarm the ecclesiastical

tical Electors, and in those fertile countries to open new resources for the prosecution of the war. He followed the course of the Maine; Seligenstadt, Aschaffenburg, Steinheim, and all the country on both sides of this river, were subjected on his march; the Imperial garrisons seldom awaited, and never maintained their posts on his arrival. Some time previous, one of his colonels had been so fortunate as to take, by surprise, the town and citadel of Hanau, upon the preservation of which, Tilly had been so intent; and eager to be freed from the yoke of the Imperialists, the Count of that name immediately put himself under the protection of the Swedish monarch.

The King's attention was now turned towards Frankfort, it being a settled maxim with him in his progress through Germany, ever to secure his rear by the friendship and possession of its principal cities. Frankfort was one of the first free cities which he had from Saxony endeavoured to prepare for his reception; and he now summoned it, by new deputies from Offenbach, to grant him a free passage. This city would have willingly preserved a neutral system between the Emperor and the King of Sweden, as, whatever party the inhabitants embraced,

embraced, they had reason to be apprehensive for their privileges and commerce; they might feel the heavy weight of Imperial indignation if they hastily submitted to the King of **Sweden, and** the latter was afterwards unable to defend them against the Emperor's despotism. But the displeasure of an irresistible conqueror was much more to be feared while he was before their gates with a formidable army, and could punish their opposition by the loss of their commerce and prosperity. It was in vain that their deputies alleged, as an excuse, the danger which their fairs, their privileges, and, perhaps, their constitution, would incur, by drawing down upon themselves, through a declaration for Sweden, the Emperor's vengeance. Gustavus Adolphus expressed his astonishment that so important a concern as the liberties of the whole Empire could be postponed in consideration of their annual fairs; and that they could, for a moment, sacrifice the great cause of their country and religion for temporal motives. He resolutely added, that having found the keys of every fortress from those of the island of Rugen to the Maine, he would also know where to discover those of Frankfort; that the safety of Germany and the freedom of its church being the sole motive of his invasion, he could not,

in

in confideration of the juftice of his caufe, fuffer any interruption of his progrefs. He was aware the people of Frankfort only fought to amufe him, and was therefore refolved to obtain their affiftance in earneft; the deputies who returned with this anfwer he clofely followed at the head of his army, and awaited before Saxenhaufen, in full order of battle, the decifion of the town-council.

If this city hefitated to fubmit to Guftavus Adolphus, it arofe merely from its apprehenfion of the Emperor; its own inclination not fuffering their balancing, for a moment, between the liberator of Germany and its oppreffor. The meafures under which Guftavus Adolphus now compelled them to declare themfelves, would leffen the guilt of their apoftacy in the Emperor's eyes, and conceal a voluntary ftep under the mafk of compulfion; the gates were opened for the King of Sweden, who led his army through this city in a magnificent proceffion, and in admirable order. A garrifon of fix hundred men was left in Saxenhaufen *; the King, with the reft of his army,

* The fuburb divided by the Maine from Frankfort. *Tranf.*

advanced

advanced the same evening before the town of
Hoechst, in the territories of Mentz, and it
surrendered to him before night.

While Gustavus Adolphus pursued his conquests upon the Maine, fortune crowned the
efforts of his generals in the north of Germany.
Rostock, Wismar, and Doemitz, the only strong
places which the Imperialists still possessed in
the dutchy of Mecklenburg, were taken by the
lawful sovereign, the Duke John Albert, assisted
by the Swedish general Achatius Tott. In vain
did the Imperial general Wolf, Count of Mansfeld, endeavour to recover the Magdeburg territories, of which the Swedes had taken possession
immediately after their victory at Breitenfeld;
he was obliged to relinquish his undertaking,
and abandon Magdeburg itself to the enemy.
The Swedish general Bannier, who, at the
head of 8000 men, remained upon the Elbe,
held that city closely blockaded, and defeated several Imperial regiments which were
sent to its relief. The Count of Mansfeld
defended it, however, with great resolution;
but his garrison being too small to make a long
resistance, he already began to reflect upon the
conditions on which he should surrender the
town, when Pappenheim arrived to his assistance,

ance, and occupied the besiegers in another quarter. Nevertheless, Magdeburg, or rather the miserable huts of which it now consisted, **was afterwards** voluntarily abandoned by the Imperialists, and immediately taken possession of by the Swedes.

The states of Lower Saxony ventured to recover themselves, after the successful undertakings of the King, from sloth, which the unfortunate Danish war had drawn upon them; through Wallenstein and Tilly. They assembled at Hamburg, where it was concerted to raise three regiments, with which it was expected they might be able to drive the Imperial garrisons from a country which they so much oppressed. The Bishop of Bremen, a relation of the King of Sweden, was not satisfied even with these measures, and assembled troops of his own, but had the misfortune soon to be compelled to lay down his arms by an Imperial general, Gronsfeld. Even George Duke of Lunenburg, though formerly colonel in the Emperor's service, now embraced the cause of Gustavus Adolphus, and raised some regiments for the service of that monarch, by which the Imperialists were occupied greatly to his advantage.

But

But a more important service was rendered the King by William Landgrave of Hesse Cassel, whose victorious arms made the greatest part of Westphalia and Lower Saxony, with the Bishopric of Fulda, and even the Electorate of Cologne, tremble. It was now remembered, that while the Landgrave came to Gustavus Adolphus's camp at Werben, two Imperial generals, Fugger and Altringer, had been detached by Tilly to Hesse Cassel, in order to chastise the first for his apostacy to the Emperor. But that prince had with manly courage resisted the enemy's arms, as well as his states bid defiance to Tilly's incendiary proclamations; and the battle of Leipzig soon delivered him from those ravages. He took advantage of their absence with as much courage as resolution; in a short time Vach, Minden, and Hoexter surrendered to him; and, alarmed by the rapidity of his progress, Fulda, Paderborn, and all the ecclesiastical territories which bordered upon Hesse Cassel. These states, terrified at his conquests, hastened by submission to disarm him, and redeemed themselves from plunder by the payment of considerable sums of money. After these fortunate undertakings, the Landgrave with his victorious army joined that of Gustavus Adolphus,

phus, and went in person to meet that monarch at Frankfort, to concert with him the plan of their future operations.

A number of princes and foreign ambassadors had assembled in that city, to congratulate Gustavus Adolphus on his progress, and either court his alliance or appease his indignation. Among these was the unfortunate abdicated King of Bohemia, and Elector Palatine, Frederic V. who was arrived from Holland to join the army of his avenger and benefactor. Gustavus showed him the unprofitable honour of receiving him as a crowned head, and endeavoured, by a respectful attention, to soften the remembrance of his misfortunes. But great as the advantages were which Frederic promised himself from the good fortune of his protector, and whatever expectations he had built upon his justice and magnanimity; the hopes of that unfortunate prince's reinstatement were as distant as ever. The inactivity and contradictory politics of the Court of England had abated the zeal of Gustavus Adolphus, and a pride which he could not always command led him here to forget the glorious duties of an avenger of oppression, in which quality he had so loudly announced

announced himself on his invasion of Germany*.

George Landgrave of Hesse Darmstadt was compelled upon this occasion, by the terror of the King's approach, to submit to the latter. The connexions of this suspicious prince with the Emperor, and his little zeal for the Protestant cause, were no secrets to the King; but the hatred of so contemptible an enemy could only excite his compassion, while his self-importance drew ridicule. As this Landgrave knew his own strength, and the political state of Germany, so little as to offer himself as mediator between both parties, Gustavus Adolphus, with humour, called him the *peace-maker*. When engaged at play, and he won from the Landgrave, he often said, "*The money afforded double satisfaction, as it was Imperial coin.*" The Landgrave was indebted for the King's lenity to his affinity with the Elector of Saxony,

---

* A poor excuse, with the author's leave. The Swedish monarch might have known that Charles I. then engaged in a quarrel with the rebellious fanatics of Scotland, and his own Parliament in England, without troops or revenues, could not possibly interfere in foreign transactions. Besides, his assistance was not required while the Swedes made such a progress. *Transl.*

whom Gustavus Adolphus had reason to suspect, and this monarch's contenting himself with the surrender of his fortress of Russelheim, and promise of observing a strict neutrality during the war. The Counts of Westerwald and Wetterau also visited the King at Frankfort, in order to conclude an alliance with him, and offer their assistance against the Spaniards, which in the end was very favourable to his cause. The town of Frankfort had reason to boast of the King's presence, who upon this occasion, by his royal authority, took their commerce under his protection, and, by the most effectual measures, restored their fairs, which had greatly suffered during the war.

The Swedish army was now reinforced by 10,000 men, which William Landgrave of Hesse Cassel had led to the King's assistance. Gustavus Adolphus had already attacked Koenigstein; Costheim and Fliershain surrendered after a short resistance; he became master of the river Maine, and boats were constructed with all possible expedition at Hoechst to transport the troops across the Rhine. These preparations filled the Elector of Mentz, Anselm Casimir, with consternation, and he could no longer entertain a doubt that
they

they were intended againſt him. As a partiſan of the Emperor, and one of the moſt active members of the League, he could expect no better treatment than his confederates, the Biſhops of Wirtzburg and Bamberg, had already experienced. The ſituation of his territories upon the Rhine made the poſſeſſion of them indiſpenſable to the enemy; and beſides, that beautiful country afforded invincible temptations to the neceſſitous army. But, too little acquainted with his own power and that of his opponent, the Elector flattered himſelf that he was in a condition to repel force by force, and, by the ſtrength of his fortifications, to reſiſt the Swediſh valour. He ordered the works of his capital to be repaired with all poſſible expedition, provided it with every neceſſary to ſuſtain a long ſiege, and received a reinforcement of 2000 Spaniards, commanded by Don Philip de Sylva. In order to prevent the approach of the Swediſh veſſels, he laid a boom acroſs the mouth of the Maine, and alſo ſunk large heaps of ſtones, and even veſſels, in that quarter. He, however, accompanied by the Biſhop of Worms, fled with his moſt precious effects to Cologne, and abandoned both his capital and his territories to the rapacity of a tyrannical garriſon. All theſe preparations, which betrayed less real courage than impotent insolence, did not prevent the Swedish army from advancing and making formidable preparations to besiege the city. While a part of the troops entered Rhinegau, cut in pieces all the Spaniards whom they found there, and raised contributions, another division laid the Catholic parts of Westerwald and Wetterau under contribution; the army had already encamped at Cassel, opposite Mentz, while Bernard Duke of Weimar, on the opposite side of the Rhine, took Ehrenfels and the Mouse Tower. Gustavus Adolphus had already taken measures to cross the Rhine, and block up Mentz upon the land side, when the progress of Tilly in Franconia suddenly recalled him from that siege, and obtained the Electorate a short repose.

The danger of the city of Nuremberg, which Tilly, during the absence of Gustavus Adolphus, had threatened with a siege, and the cruel fate of Magdeburg, had occasioned the King suddenly to retire from before Mentz. In order to avoid a second time the shame and the reproach of abandoning his confederates to a ferocious enemy, he hastened by rapid marches to relieve that important city; but on his arrival

at

at Frankfort, hearing the spirited resistance of the inhabitants of Nuremberg, and the retreat of Tilly, he lost not a moment to prosecute his designs against Mentz. As he failed in an attempt to pass the Rhine at Cassel under the cannon of that place, he now advanced upon the mountain road, seized every post of importance on his march, and made his appearance upon the banks of the Rhine a second time at Stockstadt, between Gernsheim and Oppenheim. The Spaniards had abandoned the mountain road, but endeavoured with obstinacy to defend the left bank of the river: they had, for this purpose, burned and sunk all the vessels in the neighbourhood, and stood in formidable force to contest with the King its passage. The King's impetuosity exposed him upon this occasion to great danger of falling into the hands of the enemy. In order to reconnoitre the opposite border, he ventured in a small boat upon the river, but had just landed when a number of Spanish cavalry fell upon him, from which he only saved himself by a precipitate retreat. At length, with the assistance of some neighbouring fishermen, he succeeded in gaining a few boats, in which he caused Count Brahe to pass at the head of 300 Swedes. No sooner had these time to intrench

trench themselves upon the opposite bank, than they were attacked by fourteen squadrons of Spanish dragoons and cuirassiers. Notwithstanding the enemy's superiority in point of number, Brahe defended himself with intrepidity, and gained time for the King in person to arrive to his assistance. The Spaniards at length retired with the loss of 600 men killed; some took refuge in Mentz, others in Oppenheim. A lion of marble, erected upon a high pillar, holding in his right claw a naked sword, and bearing on his head a casque, showed the traveller, so late as seventy years after this event, the spot where this immortal king passed the first river of Germany.

Immediately after this fortunate event, Gustavus Adolphus transported his artillery, with the greater part of his army, over the river, and besieged Oppenheim, which, after a desperate resistance, was, on the 8th of December 1631, taken by storm; 500 Spaniards, who had so courageously defended the place, fell indiscriminately a sacrifice to the Swedish fury. The intelligence of Gustavus's passing the Rhine spread consternation among the Spaniards and the troops of Lorrain, who hoped upon the left bank of that river to avoid the

the vengeance of the Swedes. Flight was now become their only refource, and every untenable place was immediately evacuated by them. After a long train of outrages upon the inhabitants, the troops of Lorrain abandoned Worms, which before their departure they wantonly ill-treated. The Spaniards haftened to fhut themfelves up in Frankenthal, where they hoped to be able to defy the victorious arms of Guftavus Adolphus.

The King now loft no time in profecuting his defigns againft the city of Mentz, into which the flower of the Spanifh troops had thrown themfelves. While he advanced againft the town upon the left bank of the Rhine, the Landgrave of Heffe Caffel had approached it upon the right, and made himfelf mafter of feveral ftrong places on his march. The befieged Spaniards, though enclofed upon every fide, difplayed in the commencement great vigour and refolution, and a fhower of bombs fell for feveral days into the Swedifh camp, which coft the King a number of brave men. Notwithftanding the vigour of this refiftance, the Swedes continually gained ground, and had advanced fo clofe to the ditch, that they entertained ferious thoughts of ftorming the place.

The

The courage of the garrison now sunk; they justly trembled for the furious impetuosity of the Swedish soldiers, of which the citadel of Marienburg in Wirtzburg afforded so dismal and recent an example; a dreadful fate awaited Mentz if taken by storm, and the enemy might easily consider himself as bound to retaliate the treatment of Magdeburg upon this rich and magnificent residence of a Catholic prince. In order rather to save the town than their own lives, the garrison capitulated the fourth day, and obtained from the magnanimity of the King a safe escort to Luxemburg: a considerable number of them, however, after the former example of others, entered the Swedish service.

On the 13th of December 1631, the King made his public entry into the conquered city, and took up his quarters in the electoral palace. Eighty cannon fell into his hands, and the inhabitants were obliged to redeem themselves from pillage by 80,000 florins. From this indulgence the Jews and clergy were excluded, who were obliged to purchase their own redemption with large sums; the Elector's library the King made a present of to his chancellor Oxenstiern, who intended to have had it transported

to

to the seminary of Westerah; but the vessel in which it was embarked for Sweden, foundered in the Baltic, and this irreparable treasure was lost.

After the loss of Mentz, fortune did not cease to persecute the Spaniards upon the Rhine. Shortly after the conquest of the latter city, the Landgrave of Hesse Cassel had taken Falkenstein and Reifenberg; Koenigstein surrendered to the Hessians; the Rhingrave Otto Louis, one of the King's generals, had the good fortune to defeat nine Spanish squadrons, who advanced from Frankenthal in order to possess themselves of the most considerable towns upon the Rhine, from Boppart to Bacharach. After the taking of the fortress of Braunfels, which the Counts of Wetterau effected with the assistance of the Swedes, the Spaniards lost every place in that country, and could preserve but few towns in the Palatinate, except Frankenthal. Landare and Cronweissenburg openly declared for the Swedes; Spires offered to raise troops for the King; Manheim was lost through the prudent measures of the young Duke Bernard of Weimar, and the negligence of its governor, who, for that misfortune, was

tried

tried before a council of war at Heidelberg, and beheaded.

The King had protracted the campaign until the depth of winter, and in all probability the severity of the season was what principally gave the Swedish soldier the advantage over his enemy. But the troops, exhausted with fatigue, now required repose in winter-quarters, which Gustavus Adolphus, soon after the surrender of Mentz, granted them in its neighbourhood. He himself took advantage of this necessary cessation of his military operations to finish, with his chancellor, the affairs of his cabinet, to treat for a neutrality with some of his enemies, and to terminate a political dispute with an allied power, which his past conduct had occasioned. He chose the city of Mentz for his winter-quarters, and for the prosecution of his state matters; and betrayed towards this place a greater partiality than appeared consistent with either the interests of the German princes, or the intended shortness of his visit to the Empire. Not contented with having extremely well fortified the town, he erected upon the opposite angle which the Maine forms with the Rhine, a new citadel, which from its founder was named Gustavusburg, but which

has

has been better known under the denomination of *Priests' Plunder.*

While Gustavus Adolphus rendered himself master of the Rhine, and threatened the neighbouring electorates with his victorious arms, his vigilant enemies made use of an artful stratagem at Paris and St. Germaine, to withdraw from him the support of France, and, if possible, to engage him in a war with **that** power. He had, by unexpectedly and suspiciously turning his arms towards the Rhine, surprised his allies, and enabled his enemies to inspire a distrust of his intentions. After he had subdued Wirtzburg and the greater part of Franconia, he could advance through Bamberg against Bavaria and Austria, and it was generally as naturally expected, that he would not delay to attack the Emperor and the Duke of Bavaria in the centre of their power, and immediately terminate the war by the subjection of these his principal **enemies**. But, to the astonishment of all, Gustavus Adolphus relinquished the warlike career which mankind had traced out for him, and instead of turning his arms to the right, advanced to the left, in order to make the more feeble princes of the Rhine feel the effects of his power, while he

gave

gave his more important adverfaries time to affemble new forces. Nothing but the expulfion of the Spaniards, in order to reinftate the unfortunate Elector Palatine, Frederic V. could make this ftrange ftep comprehenfible, and the general belief of his intended reinftalment at firft filenced the fufpicion of his friends and the calumnies of his enemies. But now the Lower Palatinate was entirely cleared of its enemies, and Guftavus Adolphus continued to purfue new plans of conqueft upon the Rhine; he even continued to retain the conquered Palatinate from its lawful fovereign. In vain did the Englifh ambaffador remind the conqueror of what equity required of him, and the duty which her folemn promife demanded of him as a man of honour; Guftavus Adolphus replied to thofe demands with bitter complaints of the inactivity of the Englifh court, and made preparations to carry his arms next into Alface, and even into Lorrain.

The diftruft of the Swedifh monarch now began loudly to declare itfelf, and the hatred of his enemies was active in fpreading unfavourable reports of his intentions. Richelieu, minifter of Louis XIII. had already taken alarm by the King's approach towards France, and the timidity

dity of his master already gave credit to the
conjectures which were uttered upon the occasion. At that period France was engaged in a
civil war with its Protestant subjects, and it
was feared, not without grounds, that the approach of a victorious king of the same religion might inspire them with new courage, and
excite them to a more desperate resistance.
This could even take place if Gustavus Adolphus was ever so removed from affording them
encouragement, and from acting unfaithfully
towards his ally the King of France. But the
vindictive spirit of the Bishop of Wirtzburg,
who sought to console himself for the loss of
his dominions at the French court, the empoi-
soned rhetoric of the Jesuits, and the forward
zeal of the Bavarian minister, represented a
private understanding between the Hugonots
and the King of Sweden as undoubted, and
found means to fill the timid disposition of
Louis with apprehensions. Not only **chimeri-**
cal politicians, but even a number of the
Catholic religion in that kingdom, believed it;
fanatic zealots already saw him prepared to pass
the Alps with an army, and dethrone even
Christ's vicegerent in Italy. Notwithstanding
the ease with which these reports of themselves
dropt so rapidly, however the tolerance and regular

lar conduct of the King made these complaints ridiculous, it was not, however, to be denied, that his undertakings upon the Rhine gave a dangerous gloss to those calumnies, as if his arms were less directed against the Emperor and the Duke of Bavaria, than against the Catholic religion itself.

The universal clamour of discontent which the Jesuits raised in all the Catholic courts against the connexions of France with the enemies of its religion, at length prevailed upon Richelieu to embrace a decisive measure for the service of the Catholic world; and at the same time to separate France from the selfishness of the Catholic states of Germany. Convinced that the intentions of the King of Sweden, like his own, were directed to humiliate the House of Austria, he spared no efforts to persuade the princes of the League to consent to a perfect neutrality, on condition that they renounced their alliance with the Emperor, and withdrew their troops from his army. In either determination of the princes Richelieu gained his ends. By their detaching themselves from the Austrian party, Ferdinand was exposed to the united arms of France and of Sweden upon every side; and Gustavus Adolphus,

phus, delivered from his other enemies in Germany, could turn his whole force againſt the hereditary dominions of the Emperor: inevitable was then the ruin of the Houſe of Auſtria, and Richelieu had gained his ends without hurting the Catholic religion. Much more dangerous were the conſequences which awaited the princes of the League, if they once oppoſed a refuſal, and perſiſted in their adherence to Auſtria. In that caſe France had juſtified its attachment to the Catholic religion before all Europe, and fulfilled its duty towards the church; the princes of the League would then appear the authors of the continual war which Germany was deſtined to wage; they alone, by their voluntary attachment to the Emperor, rendered abortive the meaſures of their protector, and drew their church into the utmoſt danger, while they expoſed themſelves to total ruin.

Richelieu followed this plan with the more zeal at a time when the repeated applications of the Elector of Bavaria for French aid cauſed him great embarraſſment. We may recollect, that ſince the period at which this prince began to doubt the Emperor's ſentiments, he had entered into a private league with France, by which

which means he thought to secure himself the Electorate Palatine, against any future alteration of conduct which the Emperor should embrace. So clearly as this treaty pointed out the enemy against whom it was directed, nevertheless did Maximilian now make a very arbitrary use of it, and did not hesitate to request from the French crown that assistance against the King of Sweden, which he had originally demanded against Austria. Embarrassed by this contradictory alliance between two opposite powers, Richelieu had now only to endeavour to put an immediate stop to their hostilities; and as little inclined to sacrifice Bavaria, as he was prevented by his treaty with Sweden from assisting it, he zealously laboured to effect a neutrality as his only means of fulfilling his engagements with both. A single plenipotentiary, the Marquis of Breze, was for this purpose sent to the King of Sweden at Mentz, in order to learn his sentiments on this head, and obtain favourable conditions for the allied princes; but Gustavus Adolphus had as powerful motives to desire the contrary, as Louis XIII. had to wish for this neutrality. Convinced by numberless proofs, that the hatred of the princes of the League towards the Protestant religion was invincible, their aversion to the foreign

foreign power of Sweden inextinguishable, and their attachment to the House of Austria irrevocable; he apprehended much less ill effects from their open hostility, than from a neutrality which stood so much in opposition to their inclinations; as he was further obliged to carry on the war in Germany at the expense of his enemies, he manifestly sustained great loss if he diminished their number without increasing that of his friends. It was therefore not surprising if Gustavus Adolphus betrayed little inclination to purchase the neutrality of the Catholic princes, at the expense of the advantages he had obtained already.

The conditions upon which he offered to accede to the Elector of Bavaria's neutrality, were accordingly severe, and pursuant to those considerations. He required from the League a total neutrality, together with withdrawing their troops from the Imperial army and all their conquests. He even demanded that the military force of the League should be diminished to a small number; that from all their territories the Imperial armies should be excluded, and assisted with neither men, provisions, nor ammunition. Hard as these conditions were, which the conquerer imposed upon the vanquished, the French mediator still flattered himself to be able to induce the Elector of Bavaria to accept them. In order to accommodate matters, Gustavus Adolphus was prevailed upon to consent to a fortnight's cessation of hostilities with the latter. But at the very period when this monarch was receiving repeated assurances from the French agent of the fortunate issue of the negotiation, an intercepted letter of the Elector to the Imperial general Pappenheim in Westphalia, discovered the perfidy of that prince, who, by the negotiation, endeavoured to gain time to defend himself. Far removed from fettering his military operations by a treaty with Sweden, that artful prince profited by the inactivity of his enemies to make the more speedy preparations; the negotiation was consequently fruitless, and only served to increase the animosity between Sweden and Bavaria.

Tilly's augmented force, with which he threatened to overrun Franconia, pressingly called the King to that circle; but he must previously expel the Spaniards, who held in check his progress towards Germany and the Netherlands, from the Rhine. With this view Gustavus Adolphus had already offered a neutrality

trality to the Elector of Treves, Philip of Zelters, under condition that the fortress of Hermanstein should be delivered to him, and a free passage granted through Coblentz. But unwillingly as the Elector beheld the Spaniards in his territories, the less disposed he was to commit his states to the suspicious protection of a heretic; as he was too weak to maintain, between two such powerful concurrents, his independence, he had recourse to the more powerful protection of France. Richelieu, with his usual policy, profited by the embarrassment of this prince to augment the power of France, and obtain an important ally upon the German frontier. A numerous French army was destined to protect the Electorate of Treves, and a French garrison was to be taken into the fortress Ehrenbreitstein. But the object for which the Elector ventured upon this bold step was not fulfilled, and the offended pride of Gustavus Adolphus was not appeased before he had obtained a free passage through the territories of Treves.

While these negotiations were carried on with France, the King's general had taken the remaining fortresses of the electorate of Mentz from the Spaniards; and Gustavus Adolphus,

by

by the capture of Creitznach, had completed the subjugation of this territory. To protect these conquests, the chancellor Oxenstern was left with a part of the forces upon the Rhine, while the great army under the King himself began its march against the enemy in Franconia.

The possession of this circle had already been disputed, with various success, between Tilly and the Swedish general Horn, whom the King had left behind with 8000 men, and the bishopric of Bamberg was in particular the scene of their ravages. After being called by his other designs to the Rhine, the King left the chastisement of the Bishop to his general, whose activity justified the choice. In a short time the entire bishopric submitted to him, and the capital, abandoned by the Imperialists, yielded to the Swedes. The banished Bishop requested assistance, in the most pressing manner, from the Elector of Bavaria, who was at length persuaded to put an end to Tilly's inactivity. Having received orders from his master to reinstate this bishop, Tilly collected the troops which were scattered through the Upper Palatinate, and marched towards Bamberg with an army of 20,000 men. Gustavus Horn, resolutely

lutely determined to maintain his conquest, awaited his arrival behind the walls of Bamberg, but saw himself constrained to yield to Tilly's vanguard what he thought to be able to dispute with his whole army. A panic which seized his troops, and which no presence of mind upon the part of their general could remedy, opened the gates to the enemy; and it was with difficulty that the troops, baggage, and artillery, were saved. The reconquest of Bamberg was the fruit of this victory; but Tilly, with all his activity, was unable to reach the Swedish general, who retired in good order behind the Maine. The appearance of the King in Franconia, whom Gustavus Horn had joined with the remainder of his troops at Kitzingen, put a stop to Tilly's conquests, and compelled him to save himself by a rapid retreat.

The King made a general review of his troops at Aschaffenburg, whose number, after his junction with Horn, Bannier, and the Duke of Weimar, amounted to near 40,000 men. His progress in Franconia was uninterrupted; for Tilly, unable to oppose so superior an enemy, had made a speedy retreat to the Danube. Bohemia and Moravia were now equally near the King, and in the uncertainty where this conqueror should direct his march, Maximilian could form no immediate resolution; the road which was now left open to Tilly must decide the King's choice, and the fate of both provinces. It was dangerous to leave Bavaria exposed in the face of so formidable an enemy, in order to cover the frontiers of Austria; it was equally dangerous, by the reception of Tilly, to invite an enemy's army into Bavaria, and make it the theatre of warlike operations. The cares of the sovereign finally overcame the stateman's scruples, and Tilly received orders, at all events, to cover the frontiers of Bavaria with his whole army.

Nuremberg received with triumphant joy the defender of the Protestant faith and of the German freedom, and the enthusiasm of the citizens expressed itself on his appearance in loud transports of admiration; Gustavus could not contain his astonishment to see himself in this city, situated in the centre of the German empire, where he never had expected to be able to penetrate: the elegant appearance of his person completed the impression which his heroic exploits had made, and the condescension with which he received the addresses of this free city, gained him in an instant the
affection

affection of all hearts. He now in person confirmed the treaty which he had concluded with its citizens upon the borders of the Baltic, and excited them to an active zeal and animosity against the common enemy. He then proceeded to the Danube, and made his appearance before the frontier town of Donauwerth*, unexpected by the enemy. A numerous Bavarian garrison defended this place, and its governor, Rodolph Maximilian Duke of Saxe Lauenburg, in the beginning showed the most resolute determination to defend it until Tilly's arrival. But the impetuosity with which Gustavus Adolphus commenced the siege, soon compelled him to think of evacuating the place, which, however, he fortunately effected amidst a tremendous fire from the Swedish artillery.

The conquest of Donauwerth made the King master of the opposite side of the Danube, and the small river Lech now only separated him from Bavaria. The immediate danger of his territories aroused all the activity of Maximilian, and, however easy he had made it for the

---

* It was not far from this town that Prince Eugene and Marlborough afterwards obtained the great victory of Blenheim. *Transl.*

enemy to approach Bavaria, he resolutely determined now to oppose their future progress. On the opposite side of the Lech, near the small town of Rain, Tilly occupied a strong position which, surrounded by three rivers, bid defiance to all attack. All the bridges on the Lech were destroyed; and its whole course as far as Augsburg, defended by strong detachments, and the possession of that free city, which had long betrayed a disposition to follow the example of Frankfort and Nuremberg, was secured by a Bavarian garrison, and the disarming of the inhabitants. The Elector shut himself up with all the troops he could assemble in Tilly's camp, seemingly resolved to place all his hopes upon this post, and set bounds to the Swedish progress.

Gustavus Adolphus soon appeared opposite the Bavarian intrenchments, after he had reduced all the territories of Augsburg, upon the hither side of the Lech, and had opened his troops a communication with that neighbourhood. It was now the month of March, when the river, swelled to an uncommon height by the great rains, and the melting snows of the mountains of Tyrol, flowed with great rapidity between steep banks. Its stream threatened

ened the rash assailant with a certain grave, and on the opposite side the enemy's cannon promised a murderous reception if he defied the fury of both the fire and the waters; and if he even passed the river, a fresh and **vigorous** enemy awaited his exhausted troops in an inaccessible camp; and instead of the refreshment so much required, his wearied **force must** attack the enemy's intrenchments, whose strength seemed to defy every power. A defeat sustained upon this river must lead the Swedes to inevitable ruin, since the same stream which set bounds to their victory, also cut off their retreat if fortune should abandon them.

The Swedish council of war which the King assembled upon this occasion, represented all these circumstances in their full force, to deter him from so dangerous an undertaking. The most intrepid were alarmed for the consequences, and a respectable warrior, grown gray under arms, did not hesitate to **express** his **doubts**. But the King's resolution was fixed. "How," said he to Gustavus Horn, who **spoke** for the rest, " what! what! after passing the Baltic, and " so many rivers in Germany, shall we be " stopped by so miserable a stream as **the** " Lech?" He had already with great danger

recon-

reconnoitred the position, and discovered that the hither side of the river was evidently more elevated than the other, by which the fire of the Swedish artillery must have the superiority over that of the enemy. With great presence of mind he profited by this circumstance. He immediately placed three batteries where the left bank of the Lech forms an angle opposite its right, and commenced a cross fire upon the enemy from seventy-two pieces of cannon. While this tremendous fire drove the Bavarians from the opposite borders, he instantly formed a bridge over the river. A thick smoke, kept up by burning wood and wet straw, concealed this operation from the enemy, while the continued thunder of artillery and the noise of axes prevented them from hearing it. He encouraged his troops by his own animating example, and himself discharged above sixty cannon. This fire was returned for two hours with equal vivacity by the Bavarians, though with less effect, as the Swedish batteries were higher situated, and served as a breastwork. It was in vain the Bavarians endeavoured to demolish the enemy's works from the opposite side; the superior fire of the Swedes put them into disorder, and they were compelled to be spectators of the finishing of the bridge. Tilly,

upon

upon this dreadful day, did the utmost to encourage his troops, and no danger could retain him from the banks of the river. At length he found the death which he sought: a cannon-ball shattered his leg, and his brave associate Altringer was soon after dangerously wounded in the head. Deprived of the encouraging presence of these two generals, the Bavarians fled, and Maximilian himself was, contrary to his wishes, led to a pusillanimous measure. Overcome by the persuasions of the dying Tilly, whose wonted resolution was overpowered by the near approach of death, he abandoned his inaccessible position; and a ford discovered by the Swedes, over which their cavalry prepared to pass, hastened his retreat. The same night, and before the Swedes had passed the Lech, he broke up his camp, and, without giving the King time to disturb his retreat, withdrew in the best order to Neuburg and Ingolstadt. With astonishment Gustavus Adolphus the next day saw his passage completed, the enemy's camp abandoned; and the Elector's flight excited his surprise more than the strength of his position. "Were I the "Bavarian," cried he, "never, even though a "cannon-ball had carried away my beard and "chin, never would I have abandoned a posi-
"tion

"tion such as this, and laid open my territories
"to the enemy."

Bavaria now lay exposed, and its territories, long spared, for the first time were subject to the ravages of war. Before, however, the King proceeded to the conquest of the enemy's country, he rescued the free city of Augsburg from the Bavarian yoke, took the citizens under his protection, and secured their fidelity by a garrison which he left; he soon after advanced by rapid marches against Ingolstadt, in order, by the capture of this important fortress, which the Elector covered with a great part of his army, to secure his conquests in Bavaria, and obtain a firm footing upon the Danube.

Shortly before his arrival in Ingolstadt had Tilly terminated his career within the walls of that city, after having experienced the utmost reverses of fortune : conquered by the superior generalship of Gustavus Adolphus, he lost, at the close of his days, the laurels of his earlier victories, and satisfied, by a chain of misfortunes, the justice of fate, and the avenging ghosts of Magdeburg. In him the Imperial army and that of the League sustained an irreparable loss, the Catholic religion was deprived of one of its

most

moſt zealous defenders, and Maximilian of Bavaria of the moſt faithful of his ſervants, who ſealed his fidelity by his death, and even performed the duty of a general in his dying moments. His laſt advice to the Elector was, to take poſſeſſion of Ratiſbon, in order to maintain the Danube, and keep open the communication with Bohemia.

With that confidence which ſo many victories naturally inſpired, Guſtavus Adolphus undertook to beſiege Ingolſtadt, and expected, by the impetuoſity of his firſt attack, to conquer all reſiſtance. But the ſtrength of its works, and the bravery of its garriſon, preſented obſtacles to him, which ſince the battle of Breitenfeld he had not met with; and a period was nearly put to his career before the walls of this city. A twenty-four pounder killed his horſe while he reconnoitred the place, but the King ſpeedily recovered, and quieted the alarms of his terrified troops by mounting another; and ſoon after his favourite, the young Margrave of Baden, was ſhot by his ſide. This warning of his evil genius was, however, diſregarded, and that inevitable death awaited him upon the plains of Lutzen, of which Ingolſtadt's walls had preſented to him the image.

The

The possession of Ratisbon by the Bavarians, who, according to Tilly's advice, had surprised this free city by stratagem, and threw into it a strong garrison, quickly changed the King's plan of operations. He had flattered himself with the hope of gaining possession of that Protestant city, and of finding in it an ally equally devoted to him with Nuremberg, Augsburg, and Frankfort. The subjection of it to the Bavarians delayed for a considerable time his favourite project of making himself master of the Danube, and cutting off the enemy's communication with Bohemia. He suddenly raised the siege of Ingolstadt, before which he wasted both his time and the lives of his men; and penetrated into the interior of Bavaria, in order, by confining the Elector to the defence of his own territories, to strip the Danube of its protectors.

The whole country as far as Munich lay open to the conqueror: Mosburg, Landshut, and the entire chapter of Freysinger, submitted to him: nothing could resist his arms. But if he met with no regular enemy, fanaticism presented him with a much more inveterate one in the bosom of every Bavarian. Soldiers who did not believe the Pope's infallibility were a new spectacle in this country. The blind zeal

of

of the priests had reprefented them to the people as monfters, children of hell, and their leader as the antichrift. It is not then furprifing if the inhabitants difpenfed with every rule of nature and humanity againft this brood of Satan, and thought themfelves juftified in the moft violent actions. Woe be to the Swedifh foldier who fingly fell into the hands of thefe barbarians! All the torments which a bigotted zeal could devife were executed upon thefe unhappy victims, and the afpect of their mangled bodies exafperated the army to exercife a dreadful retaliation. Guftavus Adolphus alone fcorned, by any act of revenge, to tarnifh the luftre of his character; and the diftruft of the Bavarians towards his religion, far from making him depart from the rules of humanity towards the unfortunate people, impofed it on him rather as a facred duty to honour his religion by the greater clemency.

The King's approach fpread terror and confternation in the capital, which, ftripped of its defenders and forfaken by its moft diftinguifhed inhabitants, fought its fafety from the conqueror's magnanimity. By an unconditional and voluntary furrender it hoped to difarm his vengeance, and already fent deputies to Freyfingen, singen, to lay at his feet the keys of the city. However the King might naturally have been led, from the inhumanity of the Bavarians, and the hostile intention of their sovereign, to abuse his victory; however pressed even by Germans to retaliate Magdeburg's fate upon the residence of its author; his great soul scorned a mean revenge, and the defenceless state of the enemy disarmed his indignation. Contented with the more noble triumph of leading the Elector Palatine, Frederic, in victorious pomp into the very residence of the prince who was the original instrument of his ruin, and the usurper of his states, he heightened the magnificence of his entry by the superior splendour of his clemency and goodness.

The King found in Munich only a forsaken palace, as the Elector's treasures had been transported to Werfen. The magnificence of the building astonished him, and he asked the guide who showed the apartments the name of the architect. "It is no other," answered the man, "than the Elector himself."—" I " would willingly have this architect to send " to Stockholm," replied the King. " That " the architect will carefully prevent," answered the other. When the arsenal was examined,

amined, the carriages were found stripped of their cannon. The latter were so artfully concealed under the floor, that no traces of them remained, and without the discovery of an artificer the deceit had not been found out. " Stand up from death," cried the King, " and " come to light." The floor was searched, and 150 pieces were discovered, some of extraordinary calibre, which had been principally taken in the Palatinate and Bohemia. A treasure of 30,000 gold ducats, found in one of the large cannon, completed the pleasure which the King received on this occasion.

But a more pleasing spectacle he would have received from the Bavarian army, to attack which in their intrenchments he had penetrated so far into the country. In this expectation the King was, however, disappointed. No enemy appeared, and the Elector could not be persuaded by the most pressing instances of his people to hazard the remainder of his army in the field of battle. Shut up in Ratisbon, he awaited the reinforcements which Wallenstein was leading from Bohemia, and in the mean time endeavoured, by a renewal of his system of neutrality, to retain his enemy from active measures. But the King's distrust, so often excited,

excited, frustrated this design, and the premeditated delay of Wallenstein abandoned the Bavarians to the fury of the Swedes.

Thus far had Gustavus Adolphus advanced from one victory to another, and from conquest to conquest, without finding an enemy capable of checking his progress. A part of Bavaria and Suabia, the bishoprics of Franconia, the Lower Palatinate, and the electorate of Mentz, lay conquered in his rear. An uninterrupted good fortune had attended him to the borders of the Austrian monarchy, and a splendid success had justified the plan of operations which he had formed immediately upon obtaining the victory at Breitenfeld. If he had not succeeded according to his desires, in promoting a confederacy among the Protestant states, he had either disarmed or weakened the Catholic League, carried on the war principally at its expense, diminished the Emperor's resources, strengthened the resolution of the weaker states, and, by laying under contribution the Imperial allies, found a way to the heart of Austria. Where he could not use the force of arms, the utmost service was rendered him by the free cities, whose affections he had gained by the double ties of religion and policy; and so long as he
main-

maintained a superiority in the field he might
form every expectation from their zeal. By
means of his conquests upon the Rhine, the
Spaniards were cut off from the Lower Palatinate, should the war in the Netherlands even
leave them sufficient strength to interfere in that
of Germany; even the Duke of Lorrain embraced a neutrality at the end of this unfortunate
campaign. After so many garrisons left behind
him during his progress through Germany, his
army was not diminished; and fresh as when he
began his march, he now stood in the centre
of Bavaria, determined and prepared to penetrate into the interior of Austria.

While Gustavus Adolphus maintained the war
with such superiority in Germany, fortune was
no less favourable to his ally, the Elector of
Saxony, in another quarter. We may remem-
ber, that at the interview held between both
these princes at Halle, after the battle of Leipzig, the conquest of Bohemia fell to the Elector
of Saxony, while it was determined the King
should advance against the territories of the
League. The first fruit which the Elector
reaped from the victory at Breitenfeld was the
reconquest of Leipzig, which was followed by
the expulsion of the Austrian troops from the entire

tire circle. Reinforced by the deserters which flocked to him from the enemy's standard, the Saxon general, Arnheim, directed his march to Lusatia, which an Imperial general, Rodolph Tiefenbach, had overrun, in order to chastise the Elector for his embracing the King's cause. He had already commenced, in this badly defended province, the usual ravages, conquered several towns, and terrified Dresden itself by his approach. But his progress was suddenly checked by an order of the Emperor to spare Saxony.

Ferdinand, too late, remembered the defective politics which had led him to reduce the Elector of Saxony to extremity, and enable the King of Sweden to compel this powerful prince to an alliance. The sacrifice which he had made by an untimely haughtiness he now wished to recover by an equally ill-timed moderation, and committed a second fault while he sought to remedy the first. To deprive his enemy of so great an ally, he renewed, through the interference of Spain, his negotiations with the Elector; and to facilitate the preliminaries, Tiefenbach was ordered to evacuate the territories of Saxony. But this consideration, on the part of the Emperor, so far from producing the

the desired effect, rather discovered his embarrassment to the Elector, who, sensible of his own importance, was the more encouraged to prosecute the advantages which he had already obtained. How could he also, without rendering himself contemptible by his ingratitude, forsake an ally to whom he had given the most sacred promises of fidelity, and to whom he was indebted for the preservation of his states, and his very electorate?

The Saxon army in Lusatia advanced into Bohemia, where a train of favourable circumstances seemed to ensure them victory. The flames of insurrection still concealed themselves under the ashes in that kingdom, the first theatre of this destructive war; and the discontent of the nation was augmented by continual oppression. On every side that unfortunate country betrayed evident marks of the most melancholy alteration. Entire estates had changed their proprietors, and groaned under the yoke of Catholic masters, whom the favour of the Emperor and of the Jesuits had enriched with the plunder of the expelled Protestants. Others had taken advantage of the public calamity, to purchase the confiscated estates for a small consideration. The blood of the principal

cipal defenders of liberty was shed upon the scaffold, and such as avoided that fate by a timely flight wandered far from their native country in misery, while the obsequious slaves of despotism enjoyed their patrimony. Still more insupportable than the oppression of these petty tyrants was the restraint of conscience which they imposed upon all the Protestants of the kingdom. No exterior danger, no opposition ever so violent on the part of the nation, no example from past experience, could deter the Jesuits from their rage for making proselytes: where fair means were ineffectual, military force was employed to bring people within the pale of the church. These violences were chiefly practised against the inhabitants of Ivachimsthal, in the frontier mountains, between Bohemia and Meissen. Two Imperial commissaries, accompanied by as many Jesuits, and fifteen musketeers, repaired to this peaceful valley to preach the evangelist of heretics. Where the rhetoric of the former was ineffectual, recourse was had to the latter, and by forcibly quartering them upon the houses, by threats of banishment and fines, it was endeavoured to seduce. But on this occasion the good cause prevailed; and the vigorous resistance of this small people obliged the Emperor

dis-

disgracefully to withdraw his mandate of conversion. The example of the court afforded the Catholics of the kingdom a pattern for their conduct, and justified every sort of oppression which they used towards the Protestants. It was then not surprising if this persecuted party sought a change of condition, and saw with pleasure the appearance of their deliverers upon the frontiers.

The Saxon army was already upon its march towards Prague. The Imperial garrisons every where retired before them. Schlukenau, Tefchen, Auflig, and Leitmeritz speedily fell into their hands, and every Catholic place was abandoned to plunder. Consternation seized all the Papists of the kingdom, and, conscious of their ill treatment of the Protestants, they were terrified on the approach of a Protestant army. All the Catholics of distinction hastily fled from the country to the capital, which they as quickly abandoned. Prague itself was prepared for no attack, and was too weakly garrisoned to sustain a long siege. The Emperor, too late, resolved to call Field-marshal Teifenbach to the defence of this capital. Before the Imperial orders could reach the head-quarters of this general in Silesia, the Saxons were already advanced

advanced near Prague, whose Protestant inhabitants promised little zeal, and whose weak garrison gave room to hope for no long resistance. In this dreadful embarrassment the Catholic inhabitants looked up to Wallenstein for their security, who now lived in Prague as a private man. But far from applying his military talents and the weight of his influence towards the preservation of the city, he rather seized the favourable moment to satiate his vengeance. If he did not immediately invite the Saxons to Prague, it was at least his conduct which facilitated its capture. Though unprepared for a long resistance, it was, nevertheless, able to defend itself until the arrival of succour: and an Imperial colonel, Count Maradas, showed a serious intention of undertaking its defence. But left without support, and having nothing to depend upon but his own courage, he durst not venture upon it without the consent of a superior: he therefore consulted Wallenstein, whose approbation might supply the place of Imperial authority, and to whom the Bohemian generals were referred in this last extremity. But he artfully adhered to his inactivity, and to his retreat from all political concerns, and thereby discouraged all the subalterns from acting. To complete the consternation,

sternation, he abandoned the capital, with his whole court, however little he had to fear from the enemy on its capture: and it immediately surrendered in consequence of his departure. His example was followed by all the Catholic nobility, the generals at the head of the troops, the clergy, and all the officers of the crown: the people were employed the whole night in saving their persons and effects: all the roads to Vienna were filled with the fugitives, who did not recover from their consternation until their arrival in the Imperial residence. Madaras himself, ready to embrace the most desperate expedients for the delivery of Prague, followed the rest, and led his small detachment to Tabor, where he awaited the event.

Profound silence reigned in Prague as the Saxons the next morning appeared before it; no measures were taken for its defence; not a shot was fired from the walls, which could announce the resistance of the Bohemians. A crowd of spectators, on the contrary, led by curiosity from the city, repaired to behold the enemy's army; and the peaceful confidence with which they approached, resembled rather a friendly welcome than a hostile reception. From the general report of those people it was known

known that the city was evacuated, and the regency fled to Budweiss. This unexpected and inexplicable want of defence excited Arnheim's distrust the more, as the speedy relief from Silesia was no secret to him, and the Saxon army was too little prepared for undertaking a regular siege, and not sufficiently numerous to take the place by storm. Apprehensive of stratagem, he redoubled his caution; and he persevered in this opinion until Wallenstein's house-steward, whom he discovered among the crowd, confirmed him in the intelligence. "The city is ours without a blow," he now cried to his officers, and immediately summoned it by a trumpeter.

The citizens of Prague, disgracefully abandoned by their defenders, had long resolved upon this measure, and they only required as a condition, the security of their liberty and property. When this was agreed to on the part of the Saxon general in his master's name, they opened their gates without resistance, and his army made their triumphal entry upon the 11th of November 1631. The Elector soon after followed, in order to receive in person the homage of those whom he newly took under his protection; for it was only under this title that the three towns of Prague had surrendered to him: this step was not to withdraw their allegiance from the House of Austria. The fears of reprisal which the Papists entertained, were the more agreeably surprised by the Elector's clemency and the strict discipline of his troops; Field-marshal Arnheim, in particular, displayed upon this occasion his consideration towards Wallenstein; not satisfied with having spared the estates of the latter in his march hither, he now placed guards upon his palace, to prevent any violence. The Catholic citizens obtained the fullest liberty of conscience, and were only deprived of four of the churches which they had taken from the Protestants. The Jesuits alone, **to whom** were attributed all former acts of oppression, were excluded from this indulgence, and banished the kingdom.

John George did not bely the subaltern pusillanimity and dependance with which the Emperor's name inspired him, and did not permit himself to pursue in Prague a conduct which would certainly be retaliated upon a future occasion in Dresden by Imperial generals such as Tilly **and** Wallenstein. He cautiously distinguished the enemy with which he waged war,

war, from the head of the Empire, whom he could respect; he did not venture to touch the house-furniture of the latter, while he appropriated to himself, without scruple, the cannon of the former, and transported them to Dresden. He did not take up his residence in the Imperial palace, but in the house of Lichtenstein, and preserved the private apartments of one whom he had deprived of a kingdom. The character of such a prince makes us doubtful whether to attribute this moderation to the self-command of discretion, or pity the weakness of a mind which good fortune itself could not inspire with boldness, **and** even liberty could not strip of its fetters.

The taking of Prague, which was soon followed by that of most **of** the other towns, operated a speedy change in the affairs of the kingdom. Many of the Protestant nobility, who had wandered about in misery, now returned to their native country; and Count Thurn, the notorious author of Bohemian insurrection, survived the triumph of beholding himself a conqueror upon the former theatre of his crime and condemnation. Over the bridge where the exposed heads of his followers terrified him by a prospect of his own fate, he

now

now made his triumphal entry, and his first care was to remove those objects of dismay; the exiles were reinstated in their properties, whose present proprietors had fled the kingdom. Disregarding the price at which estates had been purchased, even though they themselves had received the payment, they seized upon every thing which had once belonged to them, and many found cause to boast of the economy of their late possessors. The land and cattle had greatly improved under the second proprietors; the apartments were decorated with the richest furniture, the cellars which they left empty were plentifully filled, their stables inhabited, and their houses provided with the necessaries of life. But distrustful of the fortune which so unexpectedly surprised them, they hastened to disencumber themselves of their uncertain possessions, and convert their immoveable into transferable property.

The appearance of the Saxons inspired all the Protestants of the kingdom with courage; and both in the country and in the capital, crowds repaired to the newly opened Protestant churches. Many whose adherence to popery was retained only by fear, now professed the

new

new doctrine, and a number of converted Catholics with joy renounced a coercive perfuasion, in order to follow the more early conviction of their confcience. All the moderation of the new regency could not contain the juft difpleafure which an ill-treated people now manifefted to the oppreffors of their confciences; their recovered rights were ufed in a violent manner, and in many places their hatred of the religion lately impofed upon them was only fatiated with the blood of its adherents.

Meanwhile the fuccour which the Imperial generals Goetz and Tiefenbach conducted from Silefia had entered Bohemia, and were joined by fome of Tilly's regiments from the Upper Palatinate. In order to difperfe them before they could be augmented, Arnheim advanced with part of the army, and made an impetuous attack upon their intrenchments at Limburg on the Elbe. After a fevere action he at length beat the enemy from their ftrong camp, not, however, without fuftaining confiderable lofs, and compelled them, by the vehemence of his fire, to retire over the Elbe, and deftroy the bridge which they had formed upon that river; but he could not prevent the Imperialifts

from

from making reprifals, nor the Croats from purfuing their ravages as far as the gates of Prague. However fplendid and promifing the appearances were under which the Saxons opened the campaign in Bohemia, the iffue by no means fulfilled the expectations of Guftavus Adolphus. Inftead of vigoroufly purfuing the advantages obtained, and forcing a paffage through Bohemia, now conquered, to the Swedifh army, and in conjunction with it to attack the Imperial power in its centre, they weakened themfelves in a war of fkirmifhes with the enemy, in which they were not always fuccefsful, and their time for more important operations was loft. But John George's fubfequent conduct betrayed the motives which deterred him from profecuting his advantages againft the Emperor, and from promoting the King of Sweden's defigns by vigorous meafures.

The Emperor had now loft the greater part of Bohemia, and the Saxons were advancing againft Auftria, while the Swedifh monarch opened himfelf a paffage to the Imperial hereditary ftates through Franconia, Suabia, and Bavaria. A long war had exhaufted the ftrength of the Auftrian monarchy, ruined the country,

country, and diminished its armies; the renown of its victories was now no more, as well as reliance upon the invincibleness, obedience, and discipline of the troops over whom the Swedish conqueror had obtained so decisive a superiority in the field. The Emperor's allies were either disarmed, or their fidelity shaken by the approach of danger; even Maximilian of Bavaria, Austria's most powerful support, appeared inclined to yield to the enticing measures of neutrality; the suspicious alliance of that prince with France had already filled the Emperor with apprehensions. The Bishops of Wirtzburg and Bamberg, with the Elector of Mentz, and the Duke of Lorrain, were either driven from their dominions, or threatened with danger. Treves was upon the point of throwing itself under the protection of France; the Spanish armies were closely engaged by the bravery of the Dutch in the Netherlands, while Gustavus Adolphus drove them back from the Rhine; and Poland was retained by its neutrality. The borders of Hungary were threatened by the Transilvanian Prince Rogotzy, the successor of Bethlen Gabor, and the inheritor of his unquiet spirit; the Porte itself prepared to take advantage of the favourable moment. Most of the Protestant states, emboldened by the

the successes of their benefactor, had taken an active part against the Emperor; all the resources which the effrontery of Tilly and Wallenstein had obtained by oppressive contributions in these territories, were now lost; the depots, magazines, and rendezvouses destroyed; and the war could no longer be maintained at the expense of others. To complete this embarrassment, the country of the Ens raised a dangerous insurrection; where the untimely zeal of the regency for making proselytes disarmed the Protestant subjects, and created commotions while the enemy already threatened the frontiers. After so long a continuance of good fortune, such splendid victories and great conquests, and so much unnecessary effusion of blood, the Austrian monarch saw himself, a second time, plunged into the same abyss which threatened him on his accession with ruin. Should Bavaria embrace a neutrality, Saxony withstand the tempting offers, and France resolve to attack Spain at the same time in the Netherlands and Catalonia, Austria's ruin would be completed, the allied powers would divide its spoils, and the German system would undergo a total change.

The entire chain of these disasters commenced with the battle of Breitenfeld, whose unfortunate

nate issue visibly discovered the approaching ruin of the Austrian monarchy, hitherto concealed under the delusion of a great name. When men reflected upon the formidable superiority which the Swedes obtained in the field, it was principally attributed to the unlimited power of their leader, who united all the strength of his party in one point, and, fettered by no higher authority, was at liberty to profit by every favourable circumstance which might promote his ends. But since Wallenstein's resignation and Tilly's defeat, the contrary was observed on the part of the Emperor and of the League: the generals wanted consideration among their troops, and the liberty of acting; the soldiers wanted obedience and discipline, the scattered corps an unanimous effect; the states wanted attachment, their leaders union, quickness of resolution, and firmness in executing their projects. It was not their superior strength, but rather their better use of it, which gave the enemy so decisive a superiority over the Emperor; Ferdinand and the League possessed the means, but not the spirit, to convert them to a proper use. Had even Tilly never lost his reputation, the distrust entertained of Bavaria did not permit the fate of the monarchy to be left in the hands of a man who never

con-

concealed his attachment to that house. Ferdinand's most pressing want was a general who possessed experience sufficient to form and command the army, and who should devote, with blind obedience, his services to the House of Austria.

Such a choice now occupied the attention of the Emperor's privy council, whose members were divided upon the subject. In order to oppose one monarch to another, Ferdinand, in the first fire occasioned by the circumstances, offered himself to be the leader of his army; but little trouble was required to overturn a resolution which arose only from despair, and which subsided upon calm reflection. But the resolution which the Emperor was prevented from embracing by the weight of administration, circumstances permitted his son, a youth of talents and fortitude, on whom the subjects of Austria already placed great expectations. Required by his birth to defend a monarchy, whose two crowns he already bore, Ferdinand III. King of Hungary and Bohemia, united, with the natural dignity of a successor to the throne, the respect of the army and the affection of the people, so necessary for him in supporting the war. It was only the beloved successor who could

could venture to lay new burdens upon the subjects; it was only his personal appearance in the army that could extinguish the pernicious jealousy which reigned among its leaders, and restore the troops to their former discipline. If the youth wanted the necessary maturity of judgment, wisdom, and military experience, which only practice could attain, a fortunate choice of counsellors and assistants, who under the cover of his name could be invested with supreme authority, would supply the deficiency.

However rational the grounds were upon which a part of the ministry supported this proposal, it received great opposition from, perhaps, the Emperor's jealousy and the desperate state of affairs. It was dangerous to entrust the fate of the monarchy to a youth so deficient of experience; it was risking too much to oppose to the greatest general of the age, a beginner whose capacity for this important post was hitherto tried by no undertaking, who had gained no reputation, and was much too feeble to inspire a dispirited army with courage: the state which a royal leader was expected to maintain with the army, would impose a new burden upon the subject. How serious a matter
was

was it, in a word, for the Prince himself to commence his political career with an office which would render him the scourge of his people, and the oppressor of his future territories!

It was not alone necessary to find a general for the army; an army must also be found for the general. Since Wallenstein's compulsory resignation, the Emperor had defended his cause more by the assistance of Bavaria and the League than by his own armies; and this dependance upon suspicious allies rendered it necessary for him to have recourse to a general of his own. But what possibility was there of raising a new army without the all-powerful aid of gold, and a victorious commander; and an army which by its discipline, warlike spirit, and expertness, could be confronted with the experienced troops of the northern conqueror? In all Europe there was only one man capable of this, and he had received a mortal affront.

The juncture had at length arrived which procured the offended pride of Wallenstein an unprecedented satisfaction. Fate itself had avenged him, and an uninterrupted series of misfortunes, which since the day of his dismissal assailed

assailed Austria, made the Emperor confess, that with this general he had lost his right arm. Every defeat of his troops renewed these wounds, and every place lost reproached the deceived monarch with his weakness and ingratitude. Sufficiently fortunate to have lost in the offended general only the leader of his armies and the defender of his states; he found, however, in him an enemy the most dangerous of all, as he was least prepared against treason.

Removed from the theatre of war, and condemned to an irksome inactivity, while his competitor gathered laurels in the field, that proud general had beheld the change of fortune with studied composure, and concealed in theatrical pomp the dark designs of his active genius. Actuated by a glowing sensibility, while he affected a contented exterior, he calmly waited the opportunity of satiating his revenge and offended honour, which approached with slow but certain steps to a conclusion. He had now forgotten all that he owed to the Emperor, and the services which he had performed the latter were alone imprinted on his imagination; his insatiable thirst for power delighted in the Emperor's ingratitude, which seemed to absolve him from every duty.

He

He now considered himself justified in a retaliation; while the measure of his exterior career was restrained, his hopes were extended, and an enthusiastic imagination lost itself in boundless designs, which in every other character but his would appear madness. However high his merits had raised him, they were overrated, and fortune had denied him no duty which was expected as a private man and a citizen; until the moment of his dismissal, his designs had received no opposition, his ambition had felt no bounds. The blow which struck him at the diet of Ratisbon, displayed the difference between voluntary and coercive power, and the disagreement of the master from the subject. Roused from the intoxication of his power by the sudden reverse of fortune, he confounded the authority which he had possessed, with that which had deprived him of it, and his ambition observed the steps which could obtain his ends. It was after seriously experiencing the supreme power that he earnestly exerted himself; the extortion which was practised towards him, rendered him a robber. Exasperated by no injury, he dedicated his services to the throne, satisfied with being the most distinguished of its defenders; and it was not till after his disgrace that he departed from the system to which he he had adhered, and desperately ventured upon his own good fortune.

Gustavus Adolphus had overrun the north of Germany, every place was conquered, and at Leipzig fell the flower of the Austrian troops. The fame of this defeat soon reached the ears of Wallenstein, who, retired in Prague to the condition of a private man, beheld at a distance the tumult of war. What filled all Catholics with consternation, announced his greatness and good fortune; it was for him that Gustavus Adolphus laboured. Scarce had the King begun to acquire a reputation by his exploits, when Wallenstein lost not a moment to court his friendship, and unite with the fortunate enemy of Austria. The banished Count Thurn, who had long devoted his services to the King of Sweden, undertook to communicate to that monarch Wallenstein's congratulations, and to propose a close alliance. Wallenstein required 15,000 men from the King, in order, by their assistance and that of the troops which he himself engaged to raise, to conquer Bohemia and Moravia, to fall upon Vienna, and to drive the Emperor to Italy. However this unexpected offer and its successive promises excited the distrust of Gustavus Adolphus, the latter
was

was too good a judge of merit to treat such an important friend with coldness. But when Wallenstein, encouraged by the favourable reception of his first offer, renewed it after the battle of Breitenfeld, and required a decisive answer, the prudent monarch hesitated to entrust his reputation to the chimerical projects of this restless character, and so large a force to the sincerity of a man who announced himself a traitor. He alleged as an excuse the weakness of his army, which must suffer in his progress through the Empire by so sensible a diminution; and lost by too great a caution, perhaps, the opportunity to put an immediate end to the war. He too late sought to renew this negotiation; the favourable moment was past, and Wallenstein's offended pride could never forgive the neglect with which he was treated.

But the King's hesitation hastened, perhaps, the breach which the nature of their characters rendered inevitable. Both born to give laws, not to receive them, they could not be united in an undertaking which, above all others, required reciprocal sacrifices. Wallenstein was *nothing*, where he was not *every thing*; he must either act with unlimited power, or not at all. So cordially did Gustavus Adolphus detest control,

control, that he was near breaking the advantageous alliance with the French court, which fettered his active genius. Each was lost to a party which he could not govern, and the latter still less formed for a state of dependance. If the imperative commands of this ally to Wallenstein were so burdensome in common operations, they must be altogether insupportable when they required a participation of the spoil. The proud monarch could not condescend to accept the assistance of a rebellious subject against the Emperor, and to reward his important services with royal munificence; he never could so much lose sight of his own dignity as to satisfy the extravagant ambition of Wallenstein; never could he recompense useful treason with a crown. It was also from him, in case all Europe remained inactive, that a formidable competitor was looked for, should Wallenstein usurp the Bohemian sceptre; and he was in all Europe the only man who could give strength to such a veto. Rendered dictator of Germany, through the means of Wallenstein, he might turn his arms against the latter, and consider himself absolved from every sense of gratitude towards the traitor. Neither could a Wallenstein find a place with such an ally; and apparently it

was

was this, not his defigns upon the Imperial throne, which made him utter, upon hearing of the King's death, the following fentence: " Fortunate it is for him and me that he is " dead! The German Empire cannot fupport " two fuch leaders."

The firft fcheme of revenge towards the Houfe of Auftria was refolved upon, but the means to execute it remained undecided. What he had failed in effecting with the King of Sweden he hoped to obtain with lefs difficulty from the Elector of Saxony. Engaged in a continual correfpondence with Arnheim, his old friend, he from this period laboured to effect an alliance with Saxony, by which he hoped to render himfelf equally formidable to the Emperor and the King. He flattered himfelf that a meafure which, if it failed with the Swedifh monarch, would be the more readily embraced by John George, the more that prince's jealoufy was excited by the power of Guftavus Adolphus; and his otherwife weak attachment to the latter was enfeebled by the great defign of the King. Should he fucceed in withdrawing Saxony from the Swedifh alliance, and, in conjunction with it, to erect a third power in the Empire, the fate of the war lay

in

in his hands; and, led by this single step, he might satiate his vengeance against the Emperor, resent the coldness of the Swedish King, and lay the foundation of his own greatness upon the ruins of both.

But whatever measures he pursued, he could not attain his ends without the support of an army altogether devoted to him. This force could not be so privately assembled without exciting the suspicion of the Imperial court, and betraying his intentions. Such an army could not previously be informed of their rebellious destination, since it was improbable that they would listen to the voice of a traitor against their legitimate sovereign. Wallenstein was, therefore, obliged publicly to recruit under Imperial authority, and to be invested by the Emperor himself with the absolute command of the troops. How could it be otherwise when he gained the command anew, and the unlimited conduct of the war? Nevertheless, neither his pride nor his interests permitted him, in person, to solicit a post whose power was limited by the Emperor, whose fears, it might naturally be expected, should render it uncontrolled. In order to make himself master of the condition upon which the supreme command must be accepted, he must wait until he
was

was invited. This was the advice he received from Arnheim, and the end for which he laboured with deep policy and reftlefs activity.

Convinced that only extreme neceffity could conquer the Emperor's irrefolution, and the hatred of Bavaria and Spain, his moft zealous enemies, he was henceforward occupied in promoting the progrefs of the enemy, and increafing his mafter's embarraffment. It was very probable, upon his invitation and encouragement, that the Saxons, already on their march to Lufatia and Silefia, turned towards Bohemia, and overran that defencelefs kingdom: the rapid conquefts there were no lefs effected by his means. Through the defpair which he excited the capital furrendered to the conquerors. In an interview which he held under pretext of negotiating a peace with the Saxon general at Kaunitz, it may be fuppofed he fealed his treafon; and the conqueft of Bohemia was, perhaps, the firft fruit of his fecret underftanding. While he took every opportunity to promote the calamities of Auftria, which were effectually increafed by the rapid progrefs of the Swedes on the Rhine, he made his adherents in Vienna expoftulate upon the public misfortune, and complain of the dif-
miffal

missal of the late general as the source of the losses which were sustained. "Had Wallen-"stein commanded, this would never have "happened," exclaimed a thousand voices; and even in the Emperor's privy council this sentiment obtained zealous adherents.

Their repeated arguments were not necessary to convince the oppressed monarch of his past fault. His dependance upon Bavaria and the League soon became insupportable to him; but, notwithstanding this dependance, he did not betray his distrust, nor hesitate, by the recall of Wallenstein, to court the favour of the Electors. But now, pressed by daily necessity, and when the weakness of the Bavarian support became visible, he no longer scrupled to lend an ear to Wallenstein's friends, and take into consideration their proposals for the reinstatement of that general. The immense riches which the latter possessed; his high reputation, and the rapidity with which, six years before, he had assembled an army of 40,000 men; the little expense with which he had maintained that formidable force; the actions which he performed at its head; the zeal, and, in a word, the fidelity he displayed for the Emperor's honour; still made a lively impression

upon

upon the monarch, and represented Wallenstein to him as the most proper instrument to restore the balance, and to save Austria, with the Catholic religion. However sensibly the Imperial pride felt its humiliation upon this occasion; however evidently he confessed it by his departure from his former measures; however painful it was to him to descend from the dignity of his situation to entreaties; notwithstanding his suspicion of the fidelity of so bitterly offended and implacable a man; notwithstanding the force with which the Spanish minister and the Elector of Bavaria expressed their displeasure at this step, necessity at length overcame every other consideration, and Wallenstein's friends were empowered to consult his sentiments, and learn the possibility of his reinstatement.

Informed of all that passed in the Emperor's cabinet to his advantage, Wallenstein possessed self-command sufficient to conceal his inward triumph and affected indifference. The moment of revenge was arrived, and his proud heart delighted to repay the Emperor's mortification in its fullest extent. With artful eloquence did he expatiate upon the fortunate lot of a private station, which he had enjoyed

since

since his retirement from the political world. Too long, he said, he had tasted the pleasures of ease and independence to make any further sacrifices to the vain phantom of glory, and the uncertain favour of princes. All his desires for greatness and power were now extinguished, and rest was the only end of his wishes. In order to betray no impatience, he declined the Emperor's invitation to his court, but repaired at the same time to Znaim in Moravia, to facilitate his negotiation.

In the commencement it was endeavoured to confine the authority which was entrusted to him by means of a superior, and thereby to satisfy the Elector of Bavaria. The Emperor's deputies, Questenberg and Werdenberg, who, as the old friends of Wallenstein, were employed in this negotiation, received orders to mention the King of Hungary for this station, who should be present at the army, and learn the art of war under Wallenstein. But the bare mention of this name threatened to destroy the negotiation. Wallenstein declared he would never admit of an associate in the command. But after they departed from this obnoxious point, the Imperial favourite and minister, Prince Eggenberg, Wallenstein's steady

steady friend, who was sent in person to him, for a long time exhausted all his eloquence to overcome the pretended aversion of the latter. "The monarch," said the minister, "had, in "Wallenstein, lost the most costly jewel in "his crown; but he had already sufficiently "repented of this compulsive and hasty step, "and his respect for him was unchangeable. "The unlimited confidence which was now "placed on his talents and fidelity gave the "most decisive proof of it, in order to remedy "the faults of his predecessors, and to change "the appearance of matters. It would be "great and noble for him to sacrifice his just "indignation to the choice of his country, and "worthy of him to oppose the warmth of his "redoubled zeal to the calumny of his enemies. "The victory over himself," ended the prince, "would crown his inestimable merits, and "render him the greatest man of the age."

Such disgraceful circumstances and flattering promises at length appeared to disarm the indignation of Wallenstein; but not until he had exhausted all his reproaches against the Emperor, and made a pompous display of his services, and humiliated the monarch who now required his assistance. As if he yielded to these confiderations alone, he confented with haughtinefs to what was the moft ardent wifh of his foul, and deigned to favour the meffenger with a ray of hope. But too far removed to relieve the Emperor's embarraffment by a full confent, he only partly fulfilled what was required of him, in order to give the greater value to his remaining fervice. He accepted the command but for three months; only to organize the army, not to lead it againft the enemy. It was by means of this formation that he intended to difplay his power and abilities, and fhow the Emperor that his prefervation depended upon Wallenftein. Convinced that an army which his name alone drew from infignificance would return to infignificance when deferted by its creator, it ferved him as a pretext to obtain the more important conceffions on the part of his mafter: and even under thefe humiliating circumftances, Ferdinand congratulated himfelf that he had made fuch an acquifition.

Wallenftein did not long delay to put the projects into execution, which all Germany thought chimerical, and Guftavus Adolphus confidered as extravagant. But the foundation of this underaking was long fince laid, and he had

had only now to set the engines in motion, which had been prepared a number of years for this purpose. Scarce had the report of Wallenstein's preparations spread itself, when crowds of warriors repaired from the extremities of the Austrian monarchy to seek their fortunes under him. Many who had fought under his standards, had been eye-witnesses to his greatness, and experienced his munificence, now came forward from obscurity to divide with him fame and spoil. The greatness of the pay which was promised attracted thousands, and the rich support which the soldiers were to receive at the expense of the peasants, was, to the latter, an invincible motive to embrace a military life, rather than suffer under their former oppression. All the Austrian provinces were invited to join in this equipment; no situation was exempted from the taxes and capitation. The Spanish court, as well as the King of Hungary, subscribed considerable sums; the ministers made valuable presents, and Wallenstein himself advanced 200,000 dollars to hasten the preparations. The poorer officers he assisted; and by his example, and splendid promises, he enlisted troops on his own account. Whoever raised a corps was its commander. In the appointment of the officers,

officers, religion made no difference; riches, bravery, and experience were confidered more than faith. Through this equal treatment of the different sects, and still more by the declaration that the present preparations did not interfere with religion, the Proteſtant ſubject was quieted, and reconciled to the public burden. At the ſame time Wallenſtein did not fail to treat, in his own name, with foreign powers for men and money. The Duke of Lorrain's alliance he a ſecond time gained to the Emperor: Poland muſt yield him Coſſacs, and Italy warlike neceſſaries. Before the end of a month the army which was aſſembled in Moravia amounted to no leſs than 40,000 men, principally drawn from Bohemia, Moravia, Sileſia, and the other provinces of Auſtria. What appeared impoſſible to all Europe, Wallenſtein had in a ſhort time effected. He had aſſembled as many thouſands as hundreds were expected, by the charm of his reputation, his gold, and his genius. Provided, to a ſuperfluity, with all warlike neceſſaries, commanded by experienced officers, and inflamed with an enthuſiaſm which promiſed victory, this new-collected army awaited only the ſignal of their leader, to ſhow themſelves, by their exploits, worthy of him.

Wal-

Wallenſtein had fulfilled his promiſe, and the army was ready to take the field: he then retired, and left the Emperor the choice of its commander. But it was as difficult to collect ſuch another force as to find a Wallenſtein for its chief. This promiſing army, the laſt hope of the Emperor, was nothing when deprived of him who raiſed it; it aroſe through Wallenſtein, and without him it ſunk, like a magical creation, into its former inſignificance. The officers were either attached to him by former ſervices, or bound to his intereſt; the regiments had been given to his relations, his creatures, and his favourites. He alone was the man to keep the extravagant promiſes which retained the troops in the ſervice. His word was the only ſecurity for every bold expectation; implicit reliance was the only bond which contained their different ſentiments. Individual good fortune was deſtroyed when any one ſwerved from the general undertaking; a blind confidence in his power the only means to excite their zeal to unanimity.

However little Wallenſtein was earneſt in his refuſal, he profited by this means to prevail upon the Emperor to grant his extravagant demands. The enemy's progreſs rendered the danger

danger daily more pressing; and its termination depended upon one man. At length the Prince of Eggenberg received orders to use his interest with his friend Wallenstein to continue the command.

He found him at Znaim in Moravia, pompously surrounded by his troops. The deputy was received by the proud subject as a suppliant. "Never," said Wallenstein, "could he trust
" to a reinstatement, which was derived from
" the Emperor's necessity, not his justice. He
" was now sought for, when the extremity
" was at its utmost, and when from his arm
" alone safety was expected; but whatever ser-
" vices he could render would soon be for-
" gotten, and the former security would pro-
" duce ingratitude. His reputation was at stake
" if he depended upon expectations by which
" he had already been deceived; as well as
" his fortune and his repose, when he succeeded
" in fulfilling what was required of him. The
" old jealousies would soon be excited, and
" **the** independent monarch would a second
" time sacrifice his faithful servant to his con-
" venience. It would be better for him vo-
" luntarily to relinquish a post which sooner
" or later the cabals of his enemies would de-
                                    " prive

"prive him of. Safety and contentment
"awaited him from a private station, and he
"had only relinquished it in order to please
"the Emperor."

Tired of this farce, the minister at length
assumed an earnest tone, and threatened his
opposition with the Emperor's indignation if
he any longer persisted in his refusal. "The
"Imperial dignity," he added, "had suffi-
"ciently condescended already, and instead
"thereby of exciting his magnanimity had only
"encouraged his insolence; should the latter
"not be contented with this sacrifice, he
"should beware of converting the suppliant
"into the master, and exasperating the monarch
"against the rebel: that as Emperor he could
"insist upon submission; and however he
"might have erred as man, he could not as
"sovereign. If Wallenstein suffered unjustly,
"he was now recompensed for all his losses.
"Did he demand a security for his person and
"dignity, the Emperor's equity would not
"refuse it him; but offended majesty could
"not descend to any apology, and the dis-
"obedience of the subject annihilated all for-
"mer merits. The Emperor in person de-
"manded his services; whatever price he set
"upon

" upon them would be granted; but he re-
" quired obedience, without which the maf-
" ter's indignation would crush the refractory
" servant."

Wallenstein, whose extensive possessions, confined within the Austrian monarchy, lay every moment exposed to the Emperor, felt this threat was not idle. But it was not fear which at length overcame his affected obstinacy; it was this tone of entreaty, which convinced him of the weakness and desperation whence it arose; and the Emperor's readiness to yield to all his demands, announced his arrival at the summit of his utmost wishes. He now yielded to the persuasions of Eggenberg, and left to him the adjustment of his demands.

It was not without apprehension the minister beheld a writing, wherein the proudest of servants prescribed laws to the proudest of masters. But however little he depended upon the discretion of his friend, the extravagant contents of this writing exceeded his boldest expectations. Wallenstein required the unlimited command of all the German armies in the pay of Spain and of Austria, and the unconfined power of rewards and punishments; neither

the

the King of Hungary nor the Emperor himself was to appear in the army, much less to exert any prerogative. The Emperor was to bestow no place, to confer no favour, to issue no letter of grace, without the consent of Wallenstein; all the confiscations in the Empire were exclusively to be at the latter's disposal. His ordinary pay was to be augmented by an Imperial estate, and another in the Empire; every Austrian province was, in case of necessity, to be opened to him if he stood in need of a retreat. He besides this demanded the dutchy of Mecklenburg upon the conclusion of the peace, as an equivalent for his being deprived of the command at any future period.

It was in vain that the minister requested of him to moderate his demands, by means of which the Emperor was deprived of the authority over his troops, and rendered dependant upon his general; the importance of his services was too plainly disclosed to him not to be master of their price. When the necessity of the exigences inclined him to yield to those demands which revenge and haughtiness first prompted him to make, the plan of future insurrection was formed, and no advantage was to be rejected. This plan required that all the

Emperor's

Emperor's authority in Germany should be transferred to his general; and this end was attained whenever Ferdinand subscribed to the latter's conditions. The use which Wallenstein intended to make of his army, very different indeed from that for which it had been entrusted to him, admitted of no divided power, still less of higher authority. In order to be master of his designs, he must previously command the destiny of the troops. Imperceptibly to subject his sovereign to himself, and to transfer to his own person the supreme authority, he must carefully remove the Emperor from the eyes of the army: hence arose his obstinate resistance to suffer no prince of Austria with the troops. The command which he was to have over all the confiscated and conquered estates in the Empire, afforded him formidable means of purchasing dependants and useful instruments, and to act the part of a dictator in Germany much more than the Emperor in time of peace. Possessed of the power to use the Austrian territories, in case of necessity, as a retreat, he also held the means of treating the Emperor in his own dominions as a prisoner, and of shaking in its centre the power of Austria. Whatever might be the consequence, he secured himself, by the conditions which he had obtained, against

every

every event from the Emperor: if circumstances favoured his designs, his agreement with Ferdinand facilitated their execution; was he, on the contrary, unfortunate, the same conditions secured him indemnity. But how could an agreement be valid which was forcibly obtained from his sovereign, and was grounded upon treason? How could he hope to bind the Emperor by a written agreement, which condemned him to death who was so rash as to force it? Nevertheless this criminal was the most indispensable man in the monarchy, and Ferdinand, though practised in dissimulation, accorded him all that he desired.

At length an Imperial army was formed which was worthy of that name; every other influence in it, even that of the Emperor himself, ceased so soon as Wallenstein assumed the commander's staff, and no authority was confirmed which did not proceed from him. From the banks of the Danube to those of the Weser and the Oder, his influence extended; a new spirit commenced to inspire the Imperial troops, and a new epocha of the war was begun; fresh hopes were entertained by the Papists, and the Protestant world saw with concern the change of affairs.

The

The greater the price at which the general was purchased, the more expectations were formed of him at the Imperial court. But Wallenstein did not hasten to fulfil these expectations; at the head of a formidable army in the neighbourhood of Bohemia, he only required to show himself there in order to overpower the exhausted force of the Saxons, and by the reconquest of that kingdom to commence a victorious career. But satisfied to molest the enemy by skirmishes of Croats, he abandoned the best part of the kingdom to plunder, and thwarted by rapid steps his own designs; his plan was, not to oppose the Saxons, but to unite with them. Entirely occupied with this idea, he remained in the commencement inactive. More to insure his designs by the means of negotiation, he left nothing untried which was likely to detach the Elector from the Swedish alliance; and Ferdinand himself being inclined to a peace with that prince, favoured the negotiation. But the great debt which Saxony owed Sweden was still too recent in their minds to permit them to be guilty of such perfidy; and had they been actually inclined to it, the equivocal character of Wallenstein, and the bad reputation of the Austrian politics, did not permit any reliance to be placed on them.

Too

Too well known, this deceitful statesman found no confidence, even on the very occasion where, perhaps, he intended to act with sincerity; and yet circumstances did not permit him to discover his secret intentions by a confession of his real motives; he therefore, unwillingly, determined to extort by force of arms what he could not obtain by negotiation. Having suddenly assembled his troops, he appeared before Prague sooner than the Saxons could relieve that city; after a short resistance the treachery of the Capucins opened the gates to one of his regiments, and the garrison, retired to the citadel, laid down their arms under disgraceful conditions. Master of the capital, he expected the more easily to promote his negotiation with the Court of Saxony; but at the very time that he renewed it with General Arnheim, he did not neglect to complete his conquest by a decisive blow. He immediately occupied the narrow passes between Auffig and Pirna, that he might cut off the retreat of the Saxons from their own country; but Arnheim's rapidity fortunately delivered him from this danger. Soon after Egra and Leitmeritz, the only remaining places possessed by the Saxons, surrendered to the conqueror; and in a shorter time than it was

was loft, the kingdom **was** reftored to its legitimate fovereign.

Lefs occupied in promoting the interefts of his mafter than his own defigns, he now laid a plan to remove the feat of war to Saxony, and to compel the Elector, by ravaging his territories, to enter into a private treaty with the Emperor, or rather with himfelf. But however little inclined to fubmit his defigns to the force of circumftances, he was now compelled to poftpone his favourite fcheme to a more preffing neceffity. While he drove the Saxons from Bohemia, Guftavus Adolphus maintained his fuperiority upon the Rhine and the Danube, and had already removed the feat of war through Franconia and Suabia to the frontiers of Bavaria. Defeated on the Lech, and deprived of his beft fupport by the death of Tilly, Maximilian earneftly entreated the Emperor to call Wallenftein to his affiftance, and, by the defence of Bavaria, to remove the danger from Auftria itfelf. In the interim he difpatched meffengers to the general, requefting a few regiments for his immediate fafety, till the army could follow with Wallenftein at its head. Ferdinand feconded this requeft with all his authority.

But

But it now appeared how much the Emperor had furrendered his perfonal authority when he yielded up the command over his troops. Indifferent towards Maximilian's entreaties, and deaf to the repeated orders of the Emperor, Wallenftein remained inactive in Bohemia, and abandoned the Elector to his fate. The remembrance of the evil fervice which Maximilian had rendered him upon a former occafion at the diet of Ratifbon with the Emperor, was deeply engraved upon his implacable difpofition, and the Elector's late attempts to prevent his reinftatement had not been kept a fecret from him. But the moment of fatisfying his vengeance was now arrived, and Maximilian feverely felt his having made the moft vindictive of men his enemy; Wallenftein declared that Bohemia ought not to be left expofed, and that Auftria could not be better protected than when the Swedifh army exhaufted itfelf before the Bavarian fortreffes. Thus, by means of the Swedes, he chaftifed his enemy, and while every place fell into their hands, he left the Elector vainly to await his arrival in Ratifbon. Not before the entire fubjugation of Bohemia had deprived him of every excufe, and the conquefts of Guftavus Adolphus in Bavaria threatened Auftria itfelf with the near approach

of

of danger, did he yield to the preſsing entreaties of the Elector and the Emperor, and determined to effect the long-expected junction with the former, which, according to the general expectation of the Catholics, would decide the fate of the campaign.

Guſtavus Adolphus, too weak to act againſt Wallenſtein's army, was apprehenſive of the union of ſuch powerful forces, and men were juſtly aſtoniſhed that he did not prevent it with more activity. It appears that he had formed too great expectations from the hatred which divided the hoſtile generals, and gave no room to hope for the co-operation of their arms; and it was too late to remedy this miſtake when the event had contradicted his wiſhes. Upon receiving the firſt certain intelligence of their deſigns, he haſtened towards the Upper Palatinate, with a view to intercept the Elector's progreſs; but the activity of the latter defeated the King's intention, and a junction of the two armies was formed at Egra.

This frontier town was choſen by Wallenſtein for the theatre of the triumph which he intended to obtain over his proud competitor. Not contented with beholding him in the condition

dition of a suppliant, he imposed on Maximilian the hard necessity of leaving his territories exposed to the enemy, and by this distant march to declare his weakness. It cost the Elector a hard struggle to thank the man for his safety, whose ruin he sought to promote; but the urgency of the case obliged him to conquer lower passions, and he was sufficient master of himself to do it.

But whatever pains it had cost to effect this junction of the two commanders, it was still more difficult to reconcile them to the conditions upon which they were to act; the entire command must be united under one head, if the end was to be attained, and no disposition was on either side shown to relinquish the supreme authority. If Maximilian depended upon his dignity of Elector, the splendour of his descent, and his consideration in the Empire, Wallenstein was not less proud of his military exploits, and the unlimited command conferred on him by the Emperor. However severe it was for the pride of the former to be obliged to serve under an Imperial subject, Wallenstein's haughtiness was no less flattered by imposing law upon such an imperious spirit; an obstinate dispute ensued, which, however, termi-

terminated to Wallenstein's advantage. The command of both armies was unlimitedly granted to the latter, particularly on the day of battle, and the disposition and routes of the army were assigned to the Elector, who reserved no more to himself than the rewards and punishments of his own troops, and to **make** whatever use of them he thought proper, whenever they did not act in conjunction with the Imperialists.

After these preliminaries they at length ventured upon an interview, but not before they had mutually promised to bury the past in oblivion; and all the ceremonies of a reconciliation were exactly observed. According to agreement, they publicly embraced in front of the armies, and made mutual professions of friendship, while malice lurked in the hearts of both. Maximilian, versed in the arts of dissimulation, had sufficient command of his countenance not to betray his true feelings; but Wallenstein's eyes declared a malicious pleasure; and the constraint which was visible in his whole deportment, showed the joy which had overpowered his haughty disposition.

The

The combined Imperial-Bavarian armies now amounted to near 60,000 men, and were mostly veterans, before whom the Swedish monarch was not in a condition to keep the field. He accordingly retreated without delay towards Franconia, so soon as an attempt to prevent their junction had **miscarried**, and awaited a decisive movement of the enemy to form his resolution. The position of the combined armies between the frontiers of Saxony and Bavaria, **did** not leave it long doubtful whether they would remove the war to the former of these countries, or repel the Swedes from the Danube, and deliver Bavaria. Arnheim had withdrawn the troops from Saxony, to make conquests in Silesia; with the secret intention, it is reasonably supposed, of facilitating Wallenstein's entrance into the electorate, and bring John George's wavering disposition to an agreement with the Emperor. Gustavus Adolphus, conceiving that Wallenstein's designs were formed against Saxony, dispatched with all haste a considerable force to the assistance of his ally, resolutely determined to follow it with his whole army whenever circumstances should require. But the movements of Wallenstein soon convinced him of his error, and the march of the Austrian army through the

the Upper Palatinate, fet the matter beyond a doubt. The queftion was now, how to provide for his own fecurity, and to maintain his exiftence in Germany, for which he muft gain refources from the fertility of his genius. The enemy's approach furprifed the King before he had time to collect his troops, fcattered through Germany, and call the allied princes to his aid. Far too weak to approach the enemy, he had no other choice left than either to throw himfelf into Nuremberg, and rifk being fhut up in that city by Wallenftein's army and ftarved to a furrender, or facrifice Nuremberg, and under the cannon of Donauwerth to await a reinforcement. Guftavus Adolphus, indifferent to every danger and hardfhip, while he obeyed the calls of humanity and honour, immediately embraced the former refolution, determined to bury himfelf and his whole army under Nuremberg's ruins, rather than confult his fafety by the facrifice of that city.

Meafures were inftantly taken to furround the city and its fuburbs with redoubts, and to form an intrenched camp. Several thoufand men immediately commenced that laborious work, and the inhabitants of Nuremberg were infpired by a heroic zeal to rifk their blood,

their

their lives, and their properties, in the common cause. The intrenchment was surrounded by a ditch eight feet deep and twelve broad; the lines were defended by redoubts and bastions, and the gates protected by half-moons. The Pegnitz river, which flows through Nuremberg, divided the camp into two semicircles, whose communication was secured by a number of bridges; above 300 pieces of cannon defended the town-wall and the intrenchments. The peasants from the neighbouring villages, and the inhabitants of Nuremberg, assisted the Swedish soldiers with so much zeal, that the army on the seventh day was prepared to enter the camp, and in a fortnight this great work was completed.

While these transactions took place without the walls, the magistrates of Nuremberg were busily occupied in filling the magazines, and collecting provisions and ammunition for a long siege. They enforced the strictest regularity, in order to preserve the health of the inhabitants, which might easily be endangered by the conflux of so many people; and in case of the necessity of supporting the King, the youth of the city was embodied and exercised, the militia considerably reinforced, and a new regi-

regiment raised, consisting of twenty-four names, according to the letters of the old alphabet. Gustavus had, meanwhile, called to his assistance his allies, William Duke of Weimar, and the Landgrave of Hesse Cassel; and ordered his generals on the Rhine and in Thuringia to hasten their march and join him as soon as possible. His army, which was encamped within the lines of the city, did not amount to more than 16,000 men, a number not equal to one third of the enemy.

The Austrians had advanced by slow marches to Neumark, where Wallenstein made a general review. At the aspect of this formidable army he could not refrain from expressing a childish rodomantade: " Within four days it " shall be known," cried he, " whether the " King of Sweden or I shall be master of the " world." He, however, performed nothing to fulfil this promise, and neglected the opportunity of totally defeating his enemy, when the latter was so rash as to form in order of battle outside his intrenchments. " Battles enough " have been fought," exclaimed Wallenstein to those who encouraged him to the attack; " it is now time to follow another method." Here it was discovered how much was gained

by

by a general whose well-grounded reputation did not require him to stake it in any rash enterprise, to which others must hasten to form themselves a character. Convinced that the enemy's despair would dearly sell the victory, while a defeat in that quarter would infallibly lead the Emperor's affairs to ruin, he resolved to exhaust the warlike impetuosity of his antagonist by a slow siege; and while he deprived him of every opportunity of displaying his courage, he took from him the advantage which had hitherto rendered him so invincible. Without making any attempt, he formed a strong camp on the hither side of the Pegnitz, opposite Nuremberg, and by his masterly position cut off from that city all communication with Franconia, Suabia, and Thuringia. Thus he held the King besieged, and flattered himself to contain in check the impetuosity of his opponent, which he did not wish to try in the field, and reduce him by the slower but more certain means of hunger.

But, too little acquainted with the strength and resources of his adversary, Wallenstein had not taken proper measures to avert a fate which he had prepared for others. The inhabitants of the neighbourhood all fled with their property,

perty, and whatever provisions remained must be obstinately contested with the Swedes. The King spared the city magazines so long as he could procure supplies from the vicinity, and the frequent skirmishes caused a continual contest between the Croats and the Swedes, of which the neighbouring country bore the most melancholy tokens; the necessaries of life must be acquired sword in hand, and no party could forage without a numerous escort; the King had recourse to the magazines of Nuremberg, but Wallenstein was obliged to provide his troops from a greater distance. A large convoy, purchased in Bavaria, was on its march to join him, and a detachment of a thousand men was sent to escort it safe into his camp. Gustavus Adolphus having received intelligence of its approach, detached a regiment of cavalry to cut off this supply, and the darkness of the night favoured the undertaking; the whole convoy fell, with the town, which it had reached, into the hands of the King; the Imperial escort was cut in pieces, near 1200 head of cattle were driven away, and the same number of bread-waggons, which could not be removed, were set on fire. Seven regiments which Wallenstein had dispatched to Altdorf to augment the escort, were routed after an

obstinate

obstinate action by the King, who had in person advanced to cover the retreat of his party, and driven, with a loss of 400 men killed, back into the Imperial camp. So many vexatious circumstances, and such a firm resistance on the part of Gustavus Adolphus, made Wallenstein repent that he had avoided a battle; the strength of the Swedish camp now rendered an attack impracticable, and Nuremberg's armed youth served the King as a nursery, from which he could supply his loss of men. The want of provisions which prevailed in the Imperial camp as well as in the Swedish, rendered it uncertain which party should be compelled first to retreat.

The hostile armies, defended by inaccessible intrenchments, remained in view during fifteen days without undertaking any more than small attacks and inconsiderable skirmishes; on both sides epidemic distempers, the natural consequence of bad nourishment and crowded people, had occasioned a greater loss of men than the sword, and this evil increased daily. At last the long-expected succour arrived in the Swedish camp, and the considerable reinforcement which the King received enabled him to obey the dictates of his native courage, and to to break the fetters which had hitherto retained him.

Pursuant to his requisition, William Duke of Weimar had assembled troops from the Lower Saxon garrisons with all possible haste, which were joined at Sewheinfurt, in Franconia, by four regiments, and soon after, at Kitzingen, by the forces from the Rhine, which the Landgrave of Hesse Cassel and the Count Palatine of Birkenfeld detached to the King's succour. The Chancellor Oxenstern undertook to conduct this united force to the place of its destination. After being joined at Windsheim by Duke Bernard of Weimar and the Swedish general Bannier, he advanced by rapid marches to Pruck and Eltersdorf, where he passed the Pegnitz, and fortunately arrived in the Swedish camp. This succour amounted to near 50,000 men, and was attended by a train of sixty pieces of cannon, and 4000 baggage-waggons. Gustavus Adolphus now saw himself at the head of an army 70,000 strong, without reckoning the militia of Nuremberg, which could, in case of necessity, bring into the field 30,000 able citizens: a formidable force, which was opposed by one no less formidable! The war now appeared ready to be decided

decided by one decisive battle, and here to have attained its termination. With anxiety divided Europe looked to the scene of action where both armies assembled in such powerful numbers.

If before the arrival of this succour a scarcity of bread was felt, that evil had increased in both camps (for Wallenstein was joined by reinforcements from Bavaria) to a terrible degree. Besides 120,000 men which were confronted to each other, and more than 50,000 horses in both armies; besides the inhabitants of Nuremberg, who exceeded in number the Swedish army, 15,000 women were reckoned in Wallenstein's camp, with as many drivers and servants: nor was the number much less in the King's. The custom of the times permitted the soldier to lead his family into the field. A number of prostitutes followed the Imperial army, and a strict care for morals in the Swedish camp promoted marriages. For the young generation, whose native country was the camp, military schools were erected, which provided an excellent race of warriors, so that the army could recruit itself in a long war. It is not surprising these wandering bands exhausted every country through which they passed, paffed, and that the neceffaries of life were rendered fcarce. All the mills of Nuremberg were not fufficient to grind corn, which every hour grew fcarcer, and 50,000 pounds of bread, which the city daily fent to the camp, only excited hunger without fatisfying it. The laudable care of the magiftrates could not prevent the greater part of the horfes from dying for want of forage; and the increafing diftempers daily fent more than a hundred men to the grave.

To terminate thefe neceffities, Guftavus Adolphus, relying upon his ftrength, left his lines on the fifty-fifth day, formed in order of battle in front of the enemy, and cannonaded Wallenftein's camp from three batteries which he had raifed upon the banks of the Rednitz. But Wallenftein remained immoveable in his intrenchments, and contented himfelf with anfwering this challenge by a diftant fire of cannon and fmall-arms. To reduce the King to ftraits by a defenfive plan, and to overcome his patience by the force of hunger, he carefully avoided a battle; and neither the remonftrances of Maximilian, the fpirit of the army, nor the enemy's reproaches, could overcome this refolution. Deceived in his expectations, and preffed by want, Guftavus Adolphus refolved solved upon an impossibility, and determined to storm the camp, which was rendered inaccessible by art and nature.

After he had entrusted his own camp to the Nuremberg militia, he advanced on St. Bartholomew's day, the fifty-eighth of his encampment, in full order of battle, and passing the Rednitz at Furt, drove the advanced posts of the enemy with ease before him; their main force stood upon the heights between the Biber and the Rednitz; and the camp, commanded by those heights, extended along the plain. The whole artillery was collected upon this eminence. Deep ditches surrounded inaccessible intrenchments, thick abattis and pointed palisades defended the approach of a height, from the summit of which calmly and at his ease Wallenstein discharged the thunder of his artillery, amid thick clouds of smoke. An effectual fire was sustained from behind the breastworks by the musketry, and a hundred pieces of cannon threatened the bold assailant with certain destruction. It was against this dangerous post that Gustavus Adolphus directed his attack, and 500 musketeers, supported by a few infantry (for many could not advance by reason of the narrowness of the position), had

the

the unprofitable honour of being the first that sacrificed their lives before the enemy. The assault was furious, the resistance obstinate: exposed to the whole fire of the enemy's artillery, and undismayed through the aspect of inevitable death, these determined warriors stormed the heights, which, in a moment, were converted to a second Hecla, and discharged among them a shower of shot: immediately upon this the heavy cavalry rushed forward between the openings which the enemy's fire made among the assailants, whose ranks at length fell into disorder, and who, after the loss of a hundred men killed, betook themselves to flight. It was to the Germans that Gustavus Adolphus yielded the fatal post of honour; and exasperated by their retreat, he now led his Finlanders to the assault, and, by their northern courage, to disgrace the German cowardice. But they also, having experienced a similar reception, yielded to the superior position of the enemy, and a new regiment relieved them with as little success; this was succeeded by a third, a fourth, a fifth, and a sixth; so that, during a ten hours action, every regiment came into fire, and was repulsed with loss. A thousand dead bodies covered the field; nevertheless Gustavus Adolphus still renewed the attack,

attack, and Wallenſtein intrepidly maintained his poſition.

Meanwhile the Imperial cavalry charged the left wing of the Swedes, which was poſted in a field, with great impetuoſity, and the combat was maintained with intrepidity and carnage on both ſides, with various ſucceſs. Wallenſtein and Bernard Duke of Weimar had each a horſe ſhot under him; the King himſelf had part of his boot taken away by a cannon-ball. The combat was maintained with equal obſtinacy until the approach of night ſeparated them. But the Swedes found themſelves too far advanced to undertake a retreat without danger. While the King ſought for an officer to convey to the regiments his order to retreat, he met Colonel Hepburn, a brave Scotſman, whoſe native courage had alone drawn him from the camp to partake the dangers of the day. Diſpleaſed with the King, who had ſome time before preferred a younger colonel to him after a dangerous action, he had formed the reſolution of quitting the ſervice. Guſtavus Adolphus now turned to him, and, paying him ſome compliments upon his bravery, requeſted him to command the regiments to retreat. " Sire," anſwered the intrepid ſoldier, " that " is

" is the only service I can render your Majesty,
" since it is accompanied with danger :" and
immediately hastened to obey his orders. In
fact, the Duke of Weimar had, during the heat
of the battle, taken possession of an eminence
which commanded the enemy; but a heavy
rain, which fell the same night, rendered its
sides so slippery that the cannon could not be
brought up, and it was accordingly abandoned.
Diffident of his good fortune, which forsook
him on this decisive day, the King did not
venture, on the following morning, to renew
the attack, and, vanquished for the first time
because he was not victor, he led back his
troops over the Rednitz. Two thousand dead,
whom he left on the field of battle, betrayed
his loss; and Wallenstein remained in his camp
unconquered.

Both armies still continued fourteen days in
view, each with a hope of first compelling its
enemy to retreat. According as provisions were
daily consumed, hunger was felt, and the soldier, rendered furious, exercised upon the people every species of oppression. The increasing
necessity had extinguished all discipline in the
Swedish camp, and the German regiments in
particular distinguished themselves by the cru-
eltics

elties which they indiscriminately practised against friends and enemies. Individual weakness could not undertake to stop their excesses, which received a sanction from the silence of inferior commanders, and who often encouraged it by their example. The King was greatly exasperated at these breaches of a discipline, upon the observance of which he had hitherto so much piqued himself, and the warm manner in which he addressed the German officers betrayed the liveliness of his emotion. " It is you, Germans," cried he, " that rob " your country, and act against your own al- " lies. As God is my judge, I detest and " cannot bear the sight of you. You neglect " my orders, and are the cause of the curses " which I receive, and of my being every " where assailed by the tears of poverty, which " exclaim that I, as a friend, create more mis- " chief than the most desperate enemy. It is " on your account that I have stripped my " crown of its treasure, and expended above " forty tons of gold*, without having received " from you that support which I reasonably

---

* A ton of gold in Sweden amounts to 100,000 rix-dollars; consequently the King's expenses must have amounted to 633,333*l*. 6*s*. 8*d*. sterling, a large sum for so poor a country as Sweden. *Transl.*

" expected.

"expected. I divided among you my all, and,
"had you obeyed my orders, should with plea-
"sure have still expended amongst you my
"future acquisitions. Your want of discipline
"convinces me of your evil intentions, what-
"ever cause I may otherwise have to applaud
"your bravery."

Nuremberg had exceeded its strength, that it might, during eleven weeks, subsist the immense number of people which had assembled around it; but its means were at length exhausted, and the King, who commanded the more numerous part, was on that account first obliged to resolve upon a retreat. The city had interred above 10,000 of its inhabitants, and Gustavus Adolphus nearly 20,000 of his soldiers, by war and sickness. The surrounding fields had been trodden down; the villages lay in ashes; the people, plundered, languished upon the highways; dead bodies infected the air; bad nourishment, with the exhalation of so many people, together with the heat of the dog-days, produced raging disorders among men and beasts; and long after the departure of the army, misery and want prevailed in the country. Affected by the general affliction, and despairing to conquer Wallenstein's obstinacy, the King broke up his camp on the

the 8th of September, and left Nuremberg, after having taken the precaution to provide that city with a sufficient garrison. He advanced in full order of battle before the enemy, which remained motionless, and did not in the least endeavour to disturb his retreat. His march was directed to Neustadt and Windsheim, where he remained five days to refresh his troops, and be in the neighbourhood of Nuremberg, should the enemy make any attempt against that city. But Wallenstein, no less exhausted, had only awaited the departure of the Swedes to begin his own. Five days after he left his camp at Zindrof, and set it on fire. A hundred columns of smoke which arose from the surrounding villages announced his retreat, and showed Nuremberg the dreadful fate which awaited it in case it was conquered. His march, which was directed towards Forcheim, was marked by the most terrible devastation; but he was too far advanced to be overtaken by the King. The latter now divided his army, which the exhausted country could no longer subsist: a part of it was left to maintain Franconia, and with the other he prosecuted in person his conquests in Bavaria.

In the mean time the Imperial-Bavarian army was advanced into the bishopric of Bamberg, where Wallenstein mustered it anew. He found this force, which so lately had consisted of 60,000 men, diminished by the sword, sickness, and desertion, to 24,000, of whom a fourth consisted of Bavarians. Thus had the camps before Nuremberg exhausted both armies without the war approaching nearer to its end, or the expectations of Europe being fulfilled by a decisive battle. The King's conquests in Bavaria were indeed for some time interrupted by the diversion at Nuremberg, and Austria secured against invasion; but by the enemy's retreat from before that city, he was left at liberty to make Bavaria once more the theatre of war. Indifferent towards the fate of that devoted country, and weary of the burden of his alliance with its Elector, Wallenstein anxiously seized the opportunity of forsaking Maximilian, and of prosecuting his favourite schemes with renewed earnest. True to his first maxim, of detaching Saxony from Sweden, he destined that country for his winter-quarters, and hoped by his destructive presence the sooner to compel the Elector to a separate peace.

No conjuncture could be more favourably chosen for this undertaking. The Saxons had fallen upon Silesia, where, in union with the Brandenburg and Swedish reinforcements, they had obtained several advantages over the Emperor's troops. Silesia was saved by the diversion which was made in the Elector's own states; and Wallenstein's plan was the more easy, as Saxony, deprived of defence by the Silesian war, lay on every side exposed to the enemy. The necessity of saving an hereditary country of Austria prevailed before the interests of the Elector of Bavaria, and, under the mask of a patriotic zeal for the Emperor, Maximilian was sacrificed. While Bavaria was abandoned to the King of Sweden, the enemy hoped to be uninterrupted in its progress in Saxony; and the increasing coldness between that monarch and the Saxon court left room to apprehend little zeal on his part for the deliverance of John George. Once more abandoned by his artful protector, the Elector of Bavaria separated from Wallenstein at Bamberg, to protect with the small remains of his troops his helpless country; and the Imperial army directed its march through Bareith and Coburg to the Thuringian forest.

An Imperial general, Holk, was already detached into Vogtland, to ravage that defenceless province with fire and fword. He was foon after followed by Gallas, another of Wallenftein's generals, and a proper inftrument for executing his inhuman orders. At length Pappenheim was recalled from Lower Saxony, to reinforce Wallenftein's army, and to complete the miferies of the country. Ruined churches, villages in afhes, harvefts deftroyed, families plundered, and affaffinations, marked the progrefs of thefe barbarians, at whofe mercy lay all Thuringia, Vogtland, and Meiffen; but thefe were only the prelude to ftill greater miferies, with which Wallenftein himfelf, at the head of the principal army, threatened Saxony. After having left behind him the moft atrocious monuments of his fury, on his progrefs through Franconia and Thuringia, he entered with his whole force the circle of Leipzig, and compelled that city, after a fhort refiftance, to furrender. His defign was to advance as far as Drefden, and, by the fubjection of the whole country, to prefcribe law to the Elector. He had already approached the Mulda, in order, with his fuperior force, to attack the Saxon army which was advanced againft him as far as Torgau, when the King of Sweden's arrival

at

at Erfurt unexpectedly altered his plan of operations. Threatened to be surrounded by the Saxon and Swedish armies, to which George Duke of Lunenburg was expected to lead reinforcements from Lower Saxony, he suddenly turned towards Merseburg, to form a junction with Pappenheim, and to repulse the approaching Swedes.

Gustavus Adolphus had been alarmed at the intrigues which Spain and Austria made use of to detach his allies from him. The more important his alliance with Saxony was, the more cause he had to apprehend the inconstancy of John George. A sincere friendship could never take place between him and the Elector; a prince who was proud of his political importance, and who was accustomed to consider himself at the head of his party, could not without displeasure behold the interference of a foreign power in the transactions of the Empire; and the reluctance with which he saw the arrival of this unwelcome stranger, could only be conquered by the extreme danger of his territories. The increasing influence of the King in Germany, his authority over the Protestant states, the evident proofs which he betrayed of his ambitious designs, and which were suffi- cient

cient to excite the attention of all the states in the Empire, raised a thousand alarms in the Elector's breast, which the Imperial emissaries knew how to nourish and increase. Every immediate act of the King's, and even the most reasonable demands which he made of the princes of the Empire, gave birth to bitter complaints from the Elector, which threatened a speedy breach; even among the generals of both armies there appeared, so often as they acted in union, marks of that jealousy which divided their sovereigns. John George's natural aversion to the war, and his still lingering attachment to Austria, favoured the efforts of Arnheim, who continued to correspond with Wallenstein, and laboured incessantly to effect a private treaty between his master and the Emperor: if his remonstrances were long disregarded, the event proved that they were not entirely without effect.

Gustavus Adolphus, naturally apprehensive of the consequences which the defection of so powerful an ally would have upon his future existence in Germany, left no means untried to prevent this disastrous step; and his remonstrances had hitherto not entirely failed. But the formidable power with which the Emperor

seconded

seconded his deceitful projects, and the calamities with which he threatened Saxony in case of refusal, might at length overcome the Elector's firmness, should his country be left exposed; and his indifference to so powerful an ally might destroy the confidence of the other powers towards the King of Sweden. This consideration prevailed upon the King to yield to the pressing entreaties of the threatened Elector, and to sacrifice for the safety of this ally his most brilliant projects. He had already resolved on making a second attack upon Ingolstadt; and the weakness of the Elector of Bavaria gave him hopes to be able to compel that exhausted enemy to a neutrality. An insurrection of the peasantry in Upper Austria opened him a passage into that country, and the Emperor's capital might be in his possession before Wallenstein had time to render it assistance. But all these splendid hopes were postponed in consideration of an ally, who neither merited such a sacrifice by his worth or good will; who, on the most pressing occasions, only sought to promote his own interests; and who was important only from the evil he could occasion, not from any services he could render. Who can refrain from indignation when he learns, that Gustavus Adolphus's march to relieve such a friend,

friend, for ever put a period to the exploits of that great hero?

He immediately assembled his troops in the circle of Franconia, and followed Wallenstein's army through Thuringia. Bernard Duke of Weimar, who was detached against Pappenheim, joined the King at Arnstadt, where he now saw himself at the head of 20,000 veteran troops. At Erfurt he took leave of his consort, who was destined to behold him again at Weissenfels, but not until he had been encircled in his shroud! Their anxious adieu foreboded an everlasting separation.

He reached Naumburg on the 1st of November 1632, before a corps detached by Wallenstein could arrive at that place. From all quarters crowds flocked from the neighbouring country to behold the hero, the avenger, and to view the great king who a year before appeared in that country as a guardian angel; loud expressions of joy every where accompanied him, and the favour of touching the sheath of his sword and the hem of his garment was anxiously sought for. The King was moved by this innocent tribute which the sincerest gratitude and admiration paid him;

" Is

"Is it not," said he to one of his attendants, "as if this people would deify me? Our affairs go on well, but I fear that divine vengeance will punish me for this idle farce, and sufficiently convince the foolish multitude of my weak mortality." How amiable does Gustavus appear before he takes his leave of us for ever! Thus hesitates the Agamemnon of Grecian tragedy to tread the purple which veneration had spread under his feet. In the summit of his fortune he still respected the judging Nemesis, and rejected a homage which belongs only to immortality.

In the mean time Wallenstein had advanced to meet the King as far as Weissenfels, determined, even though it should cost a battle, to maintain his winter-quarters in Saxony. His inactivity before Nuremberg exposed him to suspicion, as if he was unwilling to risk a contest with the northern hero, and his reputation was endangered should he a second time avoid a battle; his present superiority of troops, though much less than during the encampment at Nuremberg, gave him the hopes of obtaining a victory if he was able to compel the King to a battle previous to the latter's junction with the Saxons. But his present reliance was not built upon the superior number of his troops, but on the assurances of his astrologer Seni, who had read in the stars that the Swedish monarch must terminate his career in the month of November*. Besides this, there were between Camburg and Weissenfels narrow defiles formed by a ridge of hills, and the river Sala, which rendered it extremely difficult for the Swedish army to advance, and could be defended by a small number of troops. The King had now no other choice but to penetrate with rapidity through these defiles, or to make his retreat through Thuringia, and to sacrifice the greater part of his troops in a desolated country, which was in want of every necessary. The diligence, however, with which Gustavus Adolphus took possession of Naumburg, rendered this plan abortive, and it was now Wallenstein himself who awaited the attack.

But he found he was deceived in this expectation, when the King, instead of advancing to Weissenfels, took every measure to intrench

* This favours a little of the marvellous; perhaps the author's admiration of Plutarch and other ancient writers, together with his theatrical turn, might have led him to adopt a tradition which, though possible, is very highly improbable. *Transf.*

himself

himself at Naumburg, and there to await the reinforcement which the Duke of Lunenburg was on the point of leading to him. Undecided whether he should advance upon the King through the narrow passes between Weissenfels and Naumburg, or remain inactive in his camp, he called a council of war to consult the opinion of his most experienced generals: none of these thought it prudent to attack the King in his advantageous position, and the preparations which the latter made to intrench his camp, plainly showed that it was not his intention soon to forsake it. But it was equally impossible to prolong the campaign on the approach of winter, and to fatigue, by continual encampments, an army which so much wanted repose: all voices declared for terminating the campaign the sooner, as the important city of Cologne, on the Rhine, was threatened with danger by the Dutch troops; and the enemy's progress in Westphalia and the Lower Rhine demanded the most effectual aid in those quarters. Wallenstein yielded to the force of these arguments; and convinced that he had no farther attack to fear on the King's part at this season of the year, he put his troops into winter-quarters, yet in such a manner as to be enabled to assemble them on the shortest notice.

notice. Pappenheim was detached with a great part of the army to the affiftance of Cologn, and had orders upon his march to take poffeffion of the fortrefs of Moritzburg near Halle. Different corps took up their quarters in the moft convenient places in the neighbourhood, that the enemy's motions might be on all fides obferved. Count Colloredo guarded the caftle at Weiffenfels, and Wallenftein with the remainder of his troops pofted himfelf near Merfeburg, between Flotzgraben and the Sala, whence his intention was to march through Leipzig, to cut off the Saxons from the Swedes.

Scarce had Guftavus Adolphus received information of Pappenheim's departure, when he inftantly broke up his camp at Naumburg, determined to fall upon the enemy, which was now weakened by one half. He advanced by rapid marches towards Weiffenfels, where the intelligence of his approach was made known to Wallenftein, who heard of it with aftonifhment; but a fudden refolution muft now be formed, and Wallenftein had taken no meafures. Although the Imperialifts could collect only 12,000 men to oppofe the enemy, which was 20,000 ftrong, yet they might expect to be

able

able to maintain their position until the return of Pappenheim, who had at furthest advanced only to Halle, five miles distant *. Messengers were instantly dispatched to recall him, and Wallenstein immediately advanced into the extensive plain which lies between the trenches and Lutzen, where he awaited the King in full order of battle, and by this position cut him off from Leipzig and the Saxon auxiliaries †.

Three cannon shots which Count Colloredo fired from the castle of Weissenfels announced the King's approach, and upon this concerted signal, Wallenstein's light troops, under the command of the Croatian General Isolani, advanced to possess themselves of the villages which lay upon the Rippach. Their weak resistance did not interrupt the enemy's march, who passed the village of Rippach (so called from the rivulet of that name), and formed above Lutzen in order of battle opposite the

* The author means German miles, each of which consists of four English. *Transf.*

† The country about Lutzen is a dead flat. The trenches which the author mentions were small canals, intended to convery timber to save land-carriage, and were impassable for cavalry and infantry. *Transf.*

Imperialsis

Imperialists. The high road which leads from Weiffenfels to Leipzig is interfected between Lutzen and Markranftadt by the trench which ftretches from Zeitz to Merfeburg, and joins the Elfter with the Sala; upon this canal were placed the left wing of the Imperialifts, and the right of the King of Sweden, but in fuch a manner that the cavalry of both armies extended themfelves upon its other fide. Wallenftein's right wing had encamped northwards behind Lutzen, and to the fouthward the left wing of the King's; both armies extended their fronts along the high road which interfected them, and divided their order of battle. But Wallenftein, to the great difadvantage of his opponent, had during the night before the engagement taken poffeffion of this road, and deepened the trenches on both fides, defending them with mufketeers, fo that they could not be paffed without difficulty and danger. Behind them was formed a battery of feven large cannon to fupport the fire of the mufketry, and feven fmaller pieces were pofted at the windmill a little behind Lutzen, upon an eminence, from whence the plain could be fwept; the infantry, divided into five large and unwieldy brigades, was formed at the diftance of three hundred yards in the rear of the high road,

road, and the cavalry covered the flanks; the baggage was sent to Lutzen, that it might not disturb the movements of the army, and the ammunition-waggons alone remained behind the line. To conceal the weakness of the Imperial forces, all the boys and drivers were mounted and joined to the left wing, and this only until the arrival of Pappenheim's troops. The entire of this order was arranged during the darkness of the night; and before day appeared, every thing was ready for the enemy's reception.

On the same night Gustavus Adolphus appeared on the opposite plain, and formed his troops in order of battle. His disposition was the same by which he had the year before conquered at Leipzig; small squadrons intercepted his line of infantry, as did musketeers that of his cavalry. The whole army was formed upon two lines, the trenches on the right and in the rear, the road in front, and the town on the left; in the centre the infantry was formed under Count Brahe, the cavalry on the wings, and the artillery in front; the left wing was entrusted to a German hero, Bernard Duke of Weimar, who commanded the German cavalry, and on the right the King led his Swedes,

Swedes, to excite the competition between both nations. The second line was formed in the same manner, and behind it was a corps of reserve under Henderson a Scotchman.

In this position they awaited the fatal morning to begin a contest which the long delay, more than the choice or the number of the troops, was destined to render bloody and decisive. The expectations of all Europe, which were disappointed in the camp before Nuremberg, were now to be satisfied on the plains of Lutzen. Two such generals so similar in consequence, in fame, and in ability, had not yet opposed each other in the whole course of the war in a decisive battle, or rendered the issue so dubious. Europe, on the following morning, was to behold its greatest general and a victor opposed to the vanquished. Although the genius of Gustavus Adolphus, or the want of talents in his opponents, conquered at Leipzig and the Lech, that question must again be debated on the following day. The morning was to decide the Emperor's choice of Wallenstein's merit, and the greatness of his services was to repay the price at which they had been purchased; each man was jealous of the reputation of his general, and under every

cuirass

cuirafs were excited thofe paffions which actuated their commander. The victory was doubtful, but the carnage was certain; each fide knew its enemy's ftrength, and the fear which was in vain endeavoured to be fuppreffed, gave a glorious proof of mutual ftrength.

Darknefs ftill covered the filent plain, and the approaching morning gave anxiety an awful delay to anticipate impending deftruction and hope. Heavy on both fides paffed the night, ftill more heavy expectation in every breaft.

At length the dreadful morning appeared; but an impenetrable fog, which fpread over the plain, ftill delayed the attack until noon. The King, in front of his army, knelt and performed his devotions; the whole army, after his example, falling on their knees, ftruck up a melodious hymn accompanied by military mufic. The King then mounted on horfeback, and only clad in a leathern doublet and a cloth coat (for a wound which he had formerly received prevented him from wearing a coat of mail), rode through the ranks to infpire the troops with a courage which the doubts of his own breaft contradicted. *God with us*, was

the

the word on the part of the Swedes; *Jesus Maria*, with the Imperialists. About eleven o'clock the fog began to disperse, and the hostile forces were in sight of each other; Lutzen at that moment was discovered on fire, which had been done by the orders of Wallenstein, that he should not be outflanked on that side. The charge was now sounded, the cavalry advanced, and the King's infantry set itself in motion against the trenches.

Received by a tremendous fire of musketry and heavy artillery, these intrepid battalions persevered in their attack; the enemy's musketeers left their posts, the trenches were passed, even the batteries were taken, and immediately turned against the Imperialists; they advanced still further with irresistible impetuosity; the first of Wallenstein's five brigades was thrown into confusion, soon after the second, and the third already began to betake itself to flight. But here Wallenstein's presence of mind exerted itself; he instantly rallied his troops, supported by three regiments of cavalry the flying brigades, formed anew, and attacked the Swedes. A murderous conflict ensued. The nearness of the enemy did not permit firing, nor the fury of the attack give any time for loading;

man

man fought againſt man, and the uſeleſs diſ-
charge of ſmall arms was exchanged for the
pike and the ſword. Overpowered by numbers, the exhauſted Swedes at length gave
way and retreated over the trenches, by which
they loſt the battery they had but juſt poſſeſſed
themſelves of; a thouſand dead bodies already
covered the plain, without any ground being
gained.

In the mean time the King's right wing, led
on by himſelf, had fallen upon the enemy's
left; the firſt ſhock of the heavy cuiraſſiers of
Finland diſperſed the lightly mounted Polanders
and Croats who had formed upon that wing,
and their diſorderly flight ſpread confuſion
and conſternation among the remainder of the
cavalry. At this moment the King was informed that his infantry had retired over the
trenches, and alſo that his left wing was thrown
into confuſion by the enemy's cannon from the
windmill. He immediately detached General
Horn in purſuit of the enemy's left, which was
defeated, while he himſelf haſtened at the head
of the regiment of Steinboc to repair the diſ-
order of his left. His noble charger immediately carried him over the trenches, but the
ſquadrons could not follow ſo quickly; and
only

only a few horsemen, among whom was Francis Albert Duke of Saxe Lauenburg, were able to keep up to the King. He flew to the spot where his infantry were in the greatest confusion, and while he looked for the place where the enemy's line could be attacked to advantage, his nearness of sight led him too close to them. An Imperial corporal remarking that the attendants every where made way for him, immediately ordered a musketeer to take his aim: " Fire at him," cried he; " that must be " a man of distinction." The soldier fired, and the King's left arm was shattered. At that moment the squadrons came up with a confused cry of, " *The King bleeds, the King is shot!*" which spread universal terror and consternation among them. " It is nothing; follow me," cried the King, collecting his whole strength; but overcome by pain, and ready to faint, he requested of the Duke of Lauenburg, in French, to lead him, without being seen, from the tumult. While the latter proceeded towards the right wing with the King, and made a long circuit to avoid exposing this discouraging spectacle to the disordered infantry, Gustavus received a second shot in the back, which deprived him of his remaining strength. " Oh, my " friend! I am gone," were his dying words:
" save

"save your own life!" He immediately fell from his horse: pierced by several shots, and abandoned by his attendants, he expired amidst the Croatian plunderers. His charger, covered with blood and flying without its master, soon convinced the Swedish cavalry of the King's fall, and they furiously rushed on to rescue this prize from the enemy; a dreadful conflict ensued about his dead body, which was buried under a heap of the slain*.

The

---

* Thus died the most accomplished of heroes; the only conqueror, perhaps, who ever made conquests in his own defence. I am far, however, from thinking he was free from ambition when he undertook the war against the Emperor. Piety (though not, perhaps, without a degree of affectation), heroic intrepidity in the field, consummate policy in the cabinet, and admirable humanity, were the leading features of a man who was more fortunate, both in his life and death, than any character of whom we read in history.

Some men have so little known him (for no good history of his exploits has hitherto appeared in England, that of Hart being by no means well executed), as to give Charles the Twelfth's victories in Poland the superiority over those of Gustavus in Germany. But besides that the former was a barbarian, whose cruelty and insolence would disgrace the most brilliant successes, he had by no means the enemy to cope with that his predecessor had; the *Muscovites* were not yet transformed into those *Russians* who, under a Munich and a Potemkin, have in our days not only been the terror

The terrible intelligence soon ran through the Swedish army; but instead of diminishing the courage of these intrepid troops, it only rendered them furious. The Swedes now thought only of revenge, and no one valued his life when the King fell; the Upland, Smaland, Finland, East and West Gothland regiments attacked the enemy's left wing a second time, which yielded to General Horn but a short resistance, and was completely beaten out of the field. Bernard Duke of Weimar now assumed the command of the Swedish army, upon the death of Gustavus Adolphus, and inspired it with the same sentiments. The left wing was immediately rallied, and attacked the right of the Imperialists with impetuosity; the artillery at the windmill, which had made so destructive a fire upon the Swedes,

---

of the Turks, but, even contrary to expectation, combated and conquered the Prussian troops, then the first in the world. Gustavus Adolphus must have been an extraordinary general to have so easily overcome the Austrians, who, though often vanquished, have been for centuries, perhaps, the most warlike people in Europe.

Had he not sullied his deeds by refusing to reinstate the unfortunate Elector Palatine, his character would, to this day, have been perfect. But what character can, above all, resist ambition, a passion rooted in all ages and conditions, and infinitely more powerful than love itself? *Transf.*

was

was taken by the Duke and turned against the
enemy; the centre also of the Swedish infantry
advanced anew under the Duke and Knyphau-
sen against the trenches, which they passed
fortunately, and a second time made themselves
masters of the battery of seven cannons. The
attack was now renewed with redoubled fury
upon the enemy's centre, which gradually resisted less and less; and even accident assisted
the bravery of the Swedes to complete the defeat: the Imperial powder-waggons blew up,
and by the terrible explosion the grenades and
bomb-shells were carried into the air. The
enemy, now in confusion, were apprehensive
of being taken in the rear, while the Swedish
brigades attacked them in front; they became spiritless, seeing their left wing beaten,
their right on the point of giving way, and
their artillery lost. The battle appeared to be
decided, and the fate of the day depended only
upon a moment: Pappenheim at this critical
juncture arrived with his cuirassiers and dragoons; every advantage gained was lost, and
the battle began anew.

The order which recalled that general to
Lutzen reached him in Halle while his troops
were employed in plundering that town. It
was

was impossible to collect the scattered infantry with the suddenness which his pressing orders and impatience required. But, without waiting for them, he ordered eight regiments of cavalry to mount, and at their head he advanced in full gallop to Lutzen. He arrived at a proper time to remedy the disorder of the Imperial left wing, which was routed by Gustavus Horn, and to engage in the combat. With rapid presence of mind he rallied the fugitives, and led them once more against the enemy. Excited by his furious impetuosity, and impatient to confront himself with the King, who, as he imagined, commanded that wing; he broke into the Swedish ranks, which, exhausted by their victory, could not oppose to him a vigorous resistance. The Imperial infantry, also exhausted, was encouraged by Pappenheim's sudden arrival, and Wallenstein immediately profited by this circumstance to form the line again. The Swedish battalions, formed in deep order, were, after a desperate conflict, repulsed over the trenches, and the twice-lost cannon a second time rescued. The entire yellow regiment, the most distinguished on this dreadful day, lay dead upon the spot which had been the scene of their intrepidity. A regiment in blue shared the same fate, which

Count

Count Piccolomini attacked with the Auſtrian cavalry and overcame after a deſperate reſiſtance. Seven different times did this intrepid general renew the attack; ſeven horſes were ſhot under him, and he was pierced by ſix muſket-balls. He neverthelefs would not quit the field of battle until led by the general retreat of the whole army. Wallenſtein himſelf was ſeen riding amid a ſhower of the enemy's bullets with cold intrepidity, encouraging the neceſſitous, applauding the brave, and intimidating the fugitives. His men fell upon each ſide of him, and his mantle was perforated by ſeveral ſhots. Another deſtiny, however, awaited him; and fate had not reſolved to terminate his career on the ſame bed with Guſtavus Adolphus.

Pappenheim, the braveſt ſoldier of the Auſtrian army and of the church, was not ſo fortunate. An ardent deſire to meet the King's perſon in battle had led him into the thickeſt tumult, where he thought he would leaſt fail of meeting his noble enemy. Guſtavus had alſo expreſſed a wiſh to encounter this reſpectable antagoniſt; but the deſires of both remained unſatisfied, and both heroes equally fell. Pappenheim was pierced by two muſket-
balls

balls in the breast, and was obliged to be taken by force from the combat. While the men were conveying him behind the line, it was whispered in his ears that he whom he sought lay dead upon the plain. When the truth of this report was confirmed his eyes sparkled with joy. " Let Wallenstein know," cried he, " that I die, not with sorrow, but, on the con-
" trary, with pleasure, since I am certain that
" the most implacable enemy of my religion
" has fallen on the same day with me."

With Pappenheim ended the fortune of the Imperialists. The cavalry, already beaten and again rallied, no sooner missed their intrepid leader than they abandoned the field of battle in disorder. The right wing fell into equal confusion, except a few regiments, which the bravery of their colonels, Goetz, Terzky, Colloredo, and Piccolomini, compelled to keep their ground. The Swedish infantry rapidly profited of the enemy's confusion. To fill up the openings which the slaughter had made, they formed both lines into one, which made the last decisive attack. A third time they crossed the trenches, and a third time took the artillery which was posted behind them. The sun was setting when both lines closed: the
action

action became warmer, and exhausted strength still endeavoured to exert itself to profit by the last precious moments of the day. It was in vain that despair displayed itself; neither side could yield, neither side could conquer; and tactics here expended all their efforts. Darkness at length put an end to the battle, which animosity would willingly have continued, because neither could find its enemy. The armies separated by a tacit agreement, the trumpets sounded, and each, claiming the victory, quitted the field.

The artillery on both sides, being abandoned by their horses, remained the whole night upon the field, as the prize of whoever should maintain it. But Wallenstein, in his haste to depart from Leipzig and Saxony, forgot to secure his part. Soon after the battle was ended, Pappenheim's infantry, consisting of six regiments which could not in sufficient time follow their general, appeared on the field; but the work was already done. A few hours earlier this considerable reinforcement might perhaps have decided the battle to the Emperor's advantage, and it was still able, by maintaining the field, to save Wallenstein's artillery, and conquer the Swedes. But there was no order for them

them to act; and, uncertain as to the issue of the battle, they retired to Leipzig, where they expected to find the army.

Wallenstein had retreated thither, where he was followed by the broken remains of his troops the next morning, without cannon, without colours, and almost without arms. It appears that the Duke of Weimar gave the Swedish army some time to repose, after the toils of this bloody day, between Lutzen and Weissenfels, sufficiently near the field of battle to oppose any attempt which the enemy should make to recover it. Of both armies, above 9000 men were killed, a still greater number were wounded; and among the Imperialists in particular scarce a man returned unhurt from the battle. The entire plain of Lutzen, as far as the trenches, was covered with the dead, the dying, and the wounded. Many of the first nobility had fallen on both sides; even the Abbot of Fulda, who had mingled himself in the combat as a spectator, paid for his curiosity and his misplaced zeal with his life. History is silent with regard to prisoners; a proof of the animosity of both armies, which neither gave nor took quarter.

Pap-

Pappenheim expired the day following at Leipzig, in consequence of his wounds; an irreparable loss for the Imperial army, which this excellent warrior so often led to victory. The battle of Prague, at which he was colonel, together with Wallenstein, opened his career. Dangerously wounded, he impetuously threw himself with a few troops upon an enemy's regiment, and lay several hours for dead under his horse in the field, until his own party discovered him while they were plundering. He conquered the rebels of Austria, though 40,000 strong, with a small detachment, in three different battles; he long delayed Tilly's defeat at Leipzig by his bravery, and carried the victorious arms of the Emperor to the Elbe and to the Weser. His impetuous disposition, which defied every danger, and was capable of any attempt, rendered him the most powerful arm in the Imperial army; but he was unfit for the supreme command. The battle of Leipzig was, according to Tilly himself, lost by his hasty ardour. He also stained his hands in blood during the storming of Magdeburg. His disposition, which had been improved by his youthful application and numerous travels, had grown ferocious under arms: on his forehead two red streaks were perceptible, with which
nature

nature had marked him at his birth: thefe appeared whenever in a paffion, even in his later years; and fuperftition eafily perfuaded itfelf that the future calling of the man was marked upon the forehead of the child. Such a fervant had the beft-grounded claims to the gratitude of both the lines of Auftria, but he did not furvive the moft brilliant mark of it. The meffenger was already on his way from Madrid to bring him the order of the Golden Fleece when death feized him at Leipzig.

Although the Te Deum of victory was fung both in the Auftrian and Spanifh territories, Wallenftein openly confeffed his defeat by the diligence with which he abandoned Leipzig, and foon after all Saxony, and renounced his intentions of taking up his winter-quarters in that country. It is true he made one more weak attempt to difpute the honour of the victory, and detached his Croats next morning to the field: but the afpect of the Swedifh army, which ftood there in order of battle, immediately difperfed thefe ravaging bands; and the Duke of Weimar, by the poffeffion of the field, and foon after by the capture of Leipzig, had an undifputed claim to the victory. –

But

But a dear victory, a melancholy triumph! It was after the fury of the battle had subsided, that the importance of the loss sustained was felt, and the joy of the victors was converted into a silent and deep melancholy. He who had led them to the charge was no more returned: he lay dead among the bodies of the common men. After a long, and almost vain, search, the royal corpse was at length discovered near the great stone which had, a century before, been seen between Lutzen and the trenches, but which, from the melancholy disaster of this day, still bears the name of the Swedish Rock. Covered with blood and wounds so as to be scarce known, trodden under horses' feet, and stripped of his decorations and his clothes, he was taken out from under a heap of the dead, conveyed to Weissenfels, and there delivered up to the lamentations of his troops and the last embraces of his queen. The first tribute was paid to vengeance; but that passion was now succeeded by affection, and displayed itself in an universal lamentation: the regret of individuals was lost in the universal sorrow. The generals, struck with stupefaction, gazed upon his bier, and all the calamities which his progress had caused were buried in oblivion *.

The Emperor, as we are informed by Kevenhuller †, displayed symptoms of great emotion upon being shown the King's doublet covered with blood, of which he had been stripped during the battle. "Willingly," exclaimed he, "had I granted the unfortunate "King a longer life, and a free retreat into his "own country, if Germany was in peace!" But when a more modern Catholic author of distinguished merit does not confirm this humane anecdote, which vanity would excite in the most unfeeling breast, and might be compared to the tears which Alexander shed for the fate of Darius, it excites in us a distrust of the merits of his hero, or, what is still worse, of his own ideas of virtue. But such praise is still much with one who wished to acquit himself of regicide!

It was scarce to be expected that the powerful inclination of men to the extraordinary

---

* His body was conveyed by his queen to Sweden, and interred at Stockholm. *Transf.*

† A monk who wrote the Emperor Ferdinand's life. *Transf.*

would leave the fate of a Guſtavus Adolphus to the common courſe of nature. The death of ſuch a formidable enemy was too important an event not to leave the oppoſite party an eaſy occaſion to expreſs a ſuſpicion of the Emperor's being capable of executing whatever promoted his intereſts. But the Emperor made uſe of a foreign army in the execution of that black deed, and it was generally believed that the aſſaſſin was Francis Albert Duke of Saxe Lauenburg. The latter's rank permitted him a free and unſuſpected acceſs with the monarch, and his dignity placed him above the ſuſpicion of treachery. It conſequently requires only to be proved that this prince was capable of ſuch an atrocity, that he was excited to it, and actually committed it.

Francis Albert, the youngeſt of four ſons of Francis Duke of Lauenburg, and related by his mother to the race of Vaſa, had, in his early days, found a favourable reception at the Swediſh court. Some impropriety which he had committed in the apartment of the Queen dowager againſt Guſtavus Adolphus, it is ſaid, drew from that fiery youth a box on the ear, which, though immediately repented of and apologiſed for in the fulleſt manner, laid the

foundation

foundation of an implacable revenge. Francis Albert afterwards entered the Imperial service, where he commanded a regiment, formed a close connexion with Wallenstein, and acted as a private negotiator at the Saxon court, which did not add to his reputation. Without any sufficient cause being assigned, he went to the Swedish camp at Nuremberg to offer himself as a volunteer. By his zeal for the Protestant cause, and a disposition apparently amiable, he gained the King's affections, who, in vain warned by Oxenstern, exhausted all his favours upon the new-comer. He soon after came to the battle of Lutzen, where he accompanied the monarch as an evil demon, and did not part until he fell. Amid the enemy's balls he was safe, because he bore a green sash, the colour of the Imperialists. He was the first who brought to Wallenstein the intelligence of the King's death. Soon after this battle he entered into the Saxon service; and at the death of Wallenstein, being accused as an accomplice of that general, he saved himself, only by changing his religion, from being executed. At length he appeared anew as commander of an Imperial army in Silesia, and died of his wounds before Schweidnitz. It requires indeed some self-command to pronounce

nounce such a character innocent; but when the atrocity of such a crime is considered, it must be acknowledged that it cannot justly be imputed to him, at least according to appearances. It is known that Gustavus Adolphus exposed himself as a common soldier in every danger, and where thousands fell he might also meet his death. How he met his fate is still a question; but in such a case above all others appearances justify us in forming at least a doubt.

By whatever hand he fell, this extraordinary destiny must appear as a work of a strange nature. History, so often occupied by ungrateful subjects, and compelled to relate the uniform consequences of human passions, is sometimes consoled by sudden appearances, by which the imagination is elevated to a higher order of things. Man truly often beholds with regret the violent interference of destiny upon such occasions, which at once deprives us of the creation of an age. But the sudden effect which is made by these unexpected circumstances afterwards gives way to the rules of reason. In this manner we are struck with Gustavus Adolphus's sudden disappearance from the political theatre,

theatre, which no human prudence could have foreseen: in one day the life and soul of his party—in the next, suddenly taken away, he forsakes it, and it remains inconsolable for his loss. The Protestants, who had formed such great expectations from their invincible leader, now saw them annihilated. But it was not the benefactor of Germany who entirely fell at Lutzen; the part which he had acted for its liberties he terminated; when he ended his brilliant career, it was taken up by others, and the spirit which he had imbibed was now put in motion of itself. The Protestant party now began to consult its own resources, and the Swedish, no longer capable of acting as an oppressive ally, returned from a first to a second part.

It is certain that the King of Sweden's ambition laboured to attain an authority in the centre of the Empire, which was inconsistent with its liberty. His aim was the Imperial throne; a dignity which, possessed by him, and supported by his activity, might have caused much greater evils than were to be feared from the House of Austria. A Protestant by birth, and by principle an enemy to the Papists; born

in

in a foreign country, and brought up in the maxims of abfolute power, he was not fo well calculated to maintain the liberty of the German ftates. The coercive homage which, among others, the city of Augfburg was obliged to render to the *Swedifh crown*, betrayed the *conqueror*, not the *deliverer* of the Empire; and that city foon became prouder of the title of a royal refidence, than that of a free Imperial city. His open defigns upon the electorate of Mentz, which he in the commencement intended to beftow on the heir apparent of Brandenburg, as a dower with his daughter Chriftina, and afterwards to his chancellor and favourite Oxenftern, unequivocally declared his intentions towards the Empire. The Proteftant princes in alliance with him had claims to his gratitude, which could only be fatisfied at the expenfe of the Catholic chapters; and perhaps a plan had already been formed to divide the conquered provinces, after the manner of the barbarian hordes who had overthrown the Roman empire, among the Swedes and Germans in the army. In his conduct towards the Elector Palatine Frederic, he had entirely belied the character of a hero, and the facred duty of a protector; the Palatinate was completely in his

his possession, and honour required him to restore this province which was rescued from the Spaniards. But by a subtlety unworthy of a great mind, and which disgraces the character of a deliverer, he eluded this duty. He regarded the Palatinate as a conquest which he had made from the enemy, and thereby imagined he was entitled to treat it at his pleasure; he therefore surrendered it as a favour, and not as a debt, to the Elector, and that as a fief of Sweden, under conditions which diminished its value by one half, and rendered that prince a despicable dependant. One of the conditions to which he made the Elector subscribe was, " That after the war he should, like the other " princes, contribute to maintain a part of the " Swedish army." This lets us immediately conceive the fate which awaited Germany from the continuance of the King's success; a sudden death secured the Empire in its liberties, and saved his own reputation if he was not disposed to suffer the mortification of seeing his allies in arms against him, and losing all the fruits of his victories in a disadvantageous peace. Saxony seemed already disposed to forsake him; Denmark beheld his progress with jealousy; even France, the most potent of his allies, was alarmed

alarmed at his growing greatnefs; and at the time when he paffed the Lech, looked around for other powers by whofe affiftance his progrefs **might be** checked, and the balance of power maintained in Europe.

BOOK

BOOK IV.

THE weak spirit of union which Gustavus Adolphus excited among the Protestant members of the Empire was dissolved upon his death; the confederacy by that event was restored to its primitive freedom, and must be formed anew. In the former case they lost all the advantages which they had acquired at the expense of so much blood, and exposed themselves to the inevitable danger of becoming the prey of an enemy, to whom, by their union alone, they were equal. Neither Sweden, nor any of the states of the Empire, could singly cope with the Emperor and the League; and by a peace under such circumstances, they might be obliged to receive laws from the enemy; union was therefore the only means by which they could either conclude a peace or continue the war. But a peace sought under

the

the present circumstances, must necessarily prove a disadvantageous one to the allied powers. The death of Gustavus Adolphus inspired the enemy with new hopes, and however evil their circumstances were after the battle of Lutzen, the death of their most formidable opponent was an event so much to the disadvantage of the confederates, and in the Emperor's favour, as to justify the latter in the most brilliant expectations, and encourage him in the prosecution of the war. Its immediate consequence must be a division among the allies; this circumstance alone was greatly in favour of the Emperor and the League, and he could not bring himself to consent to a peace which was not entirely to his own advantage, nor by its means to unite the confederates. The most natural measure to be taken was, therefore, the continuation of the war, and union was acknowledged as its surest support.

But how was this union to be renewed? How were the means to be acquired for continuing the war? It was not the power of Sweden, but the talents and personal influence of its late king, which were so formidable; and it was with the utmost difficulty that he could form a small confederacy among the states.

With

With him died every thing which his influence had excited, and the mutual attachment of the states was diffolved; feveral of them already threw off a yoke which was become irkfome; others haftened to refume the authority which they could not difpute with Guftavus Adolphus during his lifetime. Some were tempted by the deceitful promifes of the Emperor; others, tired of the calamities of a fourteen years war, were fatisfied to conclude any peace whatfoever; the generals of the armies, feveral of them German princes, no longer obeyed a chief, and no one would demean himfelf fo far as to ferve under another. All union was diffolved both in the cabinet and the field, and the common caufe was in danger of being loft.

Guftavus had left no male heirs to the crown of Sweden; his daughter Chriftina, then fix years old, was the natural heir. The many defects of a regency ill agreed with that activity which Sweden muft exert under its prefent circumftances; the creative genius of Guftavus Adolphus had brought this feeble and little known country into a rank among the powers of Europe which it had not hitherto poffeffed, and from which it could not now recede with-

out

out a shameful confession of its weakness. Although the German war was principally maintained at the expense of Germany, yet the small addition which Sweden made in men and money exhausted the finances of that poor kingdom, and the subject groaned under the burden which was necessarily imposed upon him: the booty gained in Germany enriched only individuals among the nobility and the military, but Sweden still continued poor. For a considerable time, it is true, the national glory rendered these burdens supportable, because the subject expected to be amply recompensed by an advantageous peace; but these hopes ended with the death of Gustavus, and the people called aloud to ease their burdens.

But Gustavus had inspired the men to whom he had left the administration of his kingdom with his own genius. However dreadful the intelligence of his death was to them, they did not lose courage, and that noble assembly displayed the spirit of old Rome when assailed by Brennus and Hannibal; the greater the price of the acquired advantages, the less could they be relinquished; the King could not be sacrificed in vain. The Swedish council of state, divided between the prosecution of a doubtful war,

war, and an advantageous though a difgraceful peace, courageoufly embraced the caufe of danger and honour; and this venerable fenate was, with furprife, feen to form the moft active preparations. Surrounded by interior as well as outward enemies, and threatened on all fides with danger, they furmounted every obftacle with as much prudence as courage, while they ftruggled for exiftence.

The deceafe of the King, and the minority of his daughter Chriftina, renewed the claims of Poland upon the Swedifh throne, and King Ladiflaus, Sigifmund's fon, fpared no intrigues to gain a party in that kingdom. On this ground the regency at Stockholm did not lofe a moment to acknowledge the title of their fix year old Queen, and to appoint a guardianfhip; all officers in the kingdom were ordered to do homage to the new princefs, every correfpondence with Poland was prohibited, and the proclamation of former kings againft Sigifmund's heirs, was confirmed by a folemn act. The alliance with the Czar of Mufcovy was carefully renewed, in order, by the affiftance of that prince, to keep Poland in check. Guftavus's death had terminated Denmark's jealoufy, and reftored the harmony between thofe

neigh-

neighbouring states. The enemy's efforts to arm Christian IV. against Sweden, were no longer listened to; and the earnest desire he had of marrying his son Ulric to the young Queen, added to the dictates of sound policy, inclined him to a neutrality. At the same time promises of friendship and support were made by England, Holland, and France; and the Swedish council of state received powerful encouragement to continue a war which had hitherto been maintained with such reputation. However France had cause to behold the King of Sweden's death with pleasure, it saw the necessity of continuing the Swedish alliance; without exposing itself to the utmost danger, it could not permit the affairs of the Swedes to go to ruin in Germany. Without receiving support, Sweden must be compelled to a disadvantageous peace with Austria, and in that case all the efforts were lost which it cost to contain that dangerous power within bounds; or, in the other case, want and necessity led the troops to provide for their own subsistence in the territories of the Catholic princes, and France would then appear as the betrayer of those states which she had taken under her protection. The death of Gustavus Adolphus, instead of terminating the French alliance with Sweden,

Sweden, rather increased it; and while it was still equally necessary to both, it was much more advantageous to the former. It was after he who had restrained the ambition of France within bounds was no more, that the latter could execute a design upon Alsace, and sell its aid the dearer to the German Protestants.

Strengthened by these alliances, secured in their interior and on their exterior by frontier garrisons and fleets, the regency did not lose a moment to continue the war; and determined to procure, in case fortune attended their arms, a German province at least, as an indemnification of their expenses. Secure amid its seas, Sweden was not much more endangered if its armies were forcibly expelled from Germany, than if they voluntarily retired from it; and the former was as honourable, as the latter measure was disgraceful. The greater the vigour displayed, the more confidence was excited among the allies, the more respect was obtained from the enemy, and the more favourable conditions were to be expected upon the conclusion of a peace; if they were too feeble to execute all the great projects of Gustavus Adolphus, his example inspired them to exert their utmost, and to yield to nothing but necessity. It is to be lamented that self-interest had so great a share in this otherwise admirable resolution! Those who did not suffer by the calamities of the war, but who were rather enriched by it, might well resolve upon its continuance; for it was the German Empire which was in the end to defray the expenses.

But the progress of these successes was retarded by the distance of the Swedish regency from the scene of action, and by the slowness which necessarily accompanies the collegial forms. A leader of abilities was requisite to manage the Swedish affairs in Germany, and be possessed of the power to regulate both war and peace according to his own disposition. This minister must be invested with a dictatorial power, and with the authority of the crown which he represented, in order to maintain its dignity, to create union among the common operations, to give his orders the greater effect, and fully to supply the place of the monarch whom he succeeded. Such a character was found in the person of Oxenstern, the chancellor and prime minister, and, what is more, the deceased King's friend, who was fully acquainted with his secrets, versed in German politics and in the different interests of Europe,

and,

and, without comparison, was the most capable of following the plan of Gustavus Adolphus.

Oxenstern was already upon his way to Upper Germany, in order to assemble the four higher circles, when he was surprised by intelligence of the King's death. Sweden had now lost its king, Germany its deliverer, and Oxenstern the author of his fortune, the friend of his soul, and the object of his ideas. But while this calamity affected him so severely, he who raised himself by the power of his genius superior to that misfortune, was the only person to remedy it; his penetration saw every obstacle which opposed his designs, and provided a remedy for them; the states' discouragement, the intrigues of hostile courts, the defection of the confederates, the jealousy of their chiefs, and the aversion of the princes to foreign influence, were all obstacles in his way. But the situation of affairs which discovered the evil, also provided him with the means of healing it; it depended upon raising the drooping spirits of the weaker states, to oppose the private machinations of the enemy, to allow for the jealousy of the more powerful confederates, to excite the friendly powers, particularly France, to activity; but before all things, to collect the ruins of the German confederacy, and unite the divided power of the Protestants by a close and durable union. The terror with which the loss of their leader inspired the German Protestants, could equally promote a close alliance with Sweden as a sudden peace with the Emperor, and it depended only upon circumstances which of those two alternatives should be embraced; all was lost by inactivity, and only the confidence he placed in himself could excite a similar sensation among the Germans. All the attempts of the Court of Austria to detach the latter from the Swedish alliance proved fruitless, when men beheld their true advantages, and began an open breach with the Emperor.

But before these measures were pursued, and the necessary points settled between the regency and its minister, a precious moment for the activity of the Swedish army was lost, of which the enemy profited to the best advantage; the Emperor had then an opportunity of totally destroying the Swedish power in Germany, had he followed the prudent counsels of Wallenstein. The latter advised him to proclaim a general amnesty, and to meet the Protestant states

states with favourable conditions. In the first consternation occasioned by the death of Gustavus Adolphus, among the party such a declaration would have had the most powerful effect, and have brought the wavering states back to the allegiance of the Emperor. But intoxicated by sudden success, and infatuated by Spanish counsels, he determined to rely upon the more brilliant issue of his arms, rejected all mediation, and hastened to augment his forces. Spain, enriched by the grant of a tenth of the ecclesiastical possessions, which the Pope consented to, supported the Emperor with considerable subsidies, negotiated in his favour with the Court of Saxony, and raised troops in Italy which were destined to be employed in Germany. The Elector of Bavaria also considerably increased his army, and the Duke of Lorrain's restless disposition did not permit him to remain quiet in this sudden favourable reverse of fortune. But while the enemy prepared to profit by the calamity which befel the Swedes, Oxenstern spared no effort to repair the disaster.

Less apprehensive of an open enemy than of the jealousy of several of his allies, he left Upper Germany, which he had secured by means

means of conquests and alliances, and hastened to prevent the Lower German states from either a total defection, or a private confederacy among them, which would have been equally pernicious to Sweden. Offended by the importance with which the Chancellor undertook the management of transactions, and exasperated in the highest degree by receiving law from a Swedish gentleman, the Elector of Saxony began anew to promote a dangerous division; and it was now a question whether to submit unconditionally to the Emperor, or to form a third party in Germany under the head of the Protestants. Similar sentiments were perceived in Ulrich Duke of Brunswic, who sufficiently expressed them by prohibiting the Swedes to recruit in his territories, and inviting the states of Lower Saxony to Lunenburg, in order to form a confederacy under him. The Elector of Brandenburg alone, jealous of the influence which Saxony had acquired in the north of Germany, showed some zeal for the interests of the Swedish crown, which he intended to procure for his son. Oxenstern, in fact, met with the best reception at the Court of John George, but empty promises of friendship and alliance were all he was able to obtain from that prince. He was more fortunate with

the

the Duke of Brunfwic, to whom he was able to fpeak in bolder terms. Sweden was then in poffeffion of the archbifhopric of Magdeburg, whofe bifhop had the power of affembling the ftates of Lower Saxony; but the Chancellor maintained the rights of his crown, and this fpirited conduct rendered the intended affembly abortive. He however failed in erecting a Proteftant confederacy, and he was obliged to content himfelf with fome few unfteady allies in the circles of Saxony, and weaker affiftance in the fouth of Germany.

While the Bavarians were in poffeffion of the Danube, an affembly of the four higher circles was appointed to meet at Hailbron, whither the deputies of twelve free cities repaired, together with a crowd of doctors, princes, counts, and other nobility; foreign powers alfo fent their ambaffadors to this meeting, France, England, and Holland; and Oxenftern appeared at it with all the fplendour of the crown which he reprefented; he opened the meeting by a fpeech, and conducted the deliberations. After he had obtained from the ftates the moft folemn promife of friendfhip, perfeverance, and union, he propofed to them to declare the Emperor and the members of the League formally

mally as enemies. But however wide the Swedes were able to render the breach between the Emperor and the states, the latter were unwilling, by so decisive a step, to exclude every way of negotiation, and put themselves entirely in the Swedish power; they thought a formal declaration of war unnecessary, and their obstinate resistance at length overcame the Chancellor. Warmer disputes arose respecting the third and principal article, which concerned the means of prosecuting the war, and the quotas which the states were to furnish; Oxenstern's maxim, to throw the principal burden upon the states, did not so well agree with the latter, who were desirous of contributing as little as possible. Here Oxenstern experienced, as thirty Emperors had done before him, that of all difficult matters, it is the hardest to obtain money from Germans. Instead of granting the necessary sums for the new armies, they expatiated upon the calamities which had been already caused, and demanded an account of the expenditure of former sums, instead of submitting to new taxes. The bad humour into which the Chancellor's demands for money had thrown the states, raised numberless difficulties; and the irregularities committed by the troops on

their

their march, and in their quarters, excited loud complaints.

Oxenstern had learned in the service of two absolute sovereigns, too little of the formalities of a republican form of constitution to be able upon this occasion to restrain his impatience. Ready to negotiate whenever he saw the necessity of it, and firm in his determination whenever he had formed it, he did not consider the want of talents in most men: naturally prompt, he was so now from policy, for every thing depended upon concealing the real weakness of Sweden under a firm tone, and instead of receiving law, to maintain the appearance of superiority. It is not therefore surprising, if, amid such perplexities of German doctors and states, he was entirely out of his sphere; and unacquainted with the slowness which distinguishes the German character in all its public deliberations, he was brought almost to despair. Without respecting a custom to which the most powerful of the Emperors were obliged to conform, he rejected all written deliberations, which were so conformable to the national slowness; he could not conceive how ten days could be spent in debating a measure which he thought
would

would have been decided upon its being firſt propoſed. However ill he treated the ſtates, he found them very complaiſant in granting his fourth motion, which concerned himſelf; when the neceſſity of appointing a director for the new confederacy was deliberated, that honour was unanimouſly voted to the Swedes, and he was humbly requeſted to take upon his enlightened underſtanding the burden of superintending the common affairs. But, to prevent his abuſing the authority conferred upon him, there were appointed, not without French inſtigation, a number of aſſiſtants, who were in reality ſpies, to regulate the expenditure of the common treaſure, the raiſing of troops, and the marching and quartering of the army. Oxenſtern long reſiſted this limitation of his authority, which rendered extremely difficult the execution of any plan requiring diligence and ſecrecy; but at length ſo far prevailed as to be uncontrolled maſter of his own meaſures in warlike matters. The Chancellor now mentioned the delicate point of indemnification, which the Swedes expected, from the gratitude of their allies, after the concluſion of the war; and he flattered himſelf he ſhould gain Pomerania, to which the views of the

the Swedes were principally directed. But he could obtain only a general promise that no party should be abandoned at a future peace. The liberality with which the states made promises to the Chancellor sufficiently shows that their caution arose not from their respect for the constitution of the Empire. They had almost voted to him the archbishopric of Mentz, which he held already in his possession as a conquest, and it was with difficulty that the French ambassador could overcome this impolitic and disgraceful measure. However Oxenstern was deceived in his expectations, he had gained the chief point, the direction of the whole, for his crown; and he made the union of the four upper circles more compact, and obtained a subsidy of 2,500,000 rix-dollars for the yearly support of the war.

So much condescension on the part of the states merited the gratitude of the Swedes. A few weeks after the death of Gustavus Adolphus, the Elector Palatine, Frederic, ended his unfortunate days by a broken heart. This prince, who has a claim to our pity, had, during eight months, continued in the court of Gustavus, and wasted in it the small remains
of

of his patrimony *. He had nearly attained the object of his desires, and had every reason to form hopes of future good fortune, when death snatched away his benefactor. But what he regarded as his greatest calamity had the best consequences for his heirs. Gustavus Adolphus might delay the restoration of his dominions, and impose hard conditions upon that gift; but Oxenstern, to whom the friendship of England, Holland, and Brandenburg, was a matter of importance, must necessarily do justice. He therefore, at this assembly at Hailbron, restored that part of the Palatinate which was already conquered, and promised to restore the future conquest to Frederic's successor; Manheim excepted, in which a Swedish garrison was to remain until the indemnification of the Swedish expenses. The Chancellor did not confine his liberality to the Elector Palatine's family; other allied princes received, though somewhat smaller, proofs of Swedish munificence, which that crown exercised with so little expense to itself. The duties of impartialty, the most sacred of the historian, compel him to this acknowledgment,

* His two sons, Princes Rupert and Maurice, soon after entered into the service of their uncle Charles I. at the commencement of the civil wars. *Transf.*

not

not much to the honour of the champions of German liberty. However the Protestant princes of Germany could boast of the justice of their cause and the purity of their zeal, they acted chiefly from interested motives; and the desire of plundering became equally violent with the fear of being plundered. Gustavus Adolphus soon discovered that he could derive more advantage from this selfishness than from a patriotic zeal, and he did not hesitate to satisfy it. Each of the confederate princes received assurances of being put in possession of either present or future conquests which should be made of the enemy, and death alone prevented him from performing this promise. What prudence recommended, the King had imposed as a necessity upon his successor; and when the latter was obliged to prolong the war, he must in such a case divide the conquests with the princes, and place all his dependance upon the general confusion which he was desirous of exciting. Thus he promised to the Landgrave of Hesse Cassel the abbacies of Paderborn, Corvey, Munster, and Fulda; Duke Bernard of Weimar, the Franconian bishoprics; and the Duke of Wirtemberg, the ecclesiastical possessions and Austrian counties which lay situated in his territories, all under the

the title of Swedish investiture. The Chancellor himself increased this strange and disgraceful spectacle for the German Empire by not being able to restrain his contempt: " Let " it be recorded," cried he once, " in our ar- " chives, that a German prince made such a " request of a Swedish gentleman, and upon " German ground."

After such preparations it was possible to take the field, and prosecute the war with fresh vigour. Soon after the victory at Lutzen the troops of Saxony formed a junction with those of Lunenburg, and having joined the Swedish army, the Imperialists were totally driven from Saxony. The united armies now divided. The Saxons directed their march towards Lusatia and Silesia, to act, with Count Thurn, against the Imperialists: a part of the Swedish army was led by the Duke of Weimar to Franconia, and another by George Duke of Brunswic, to Lower Saxony and Westphalia.

The conquests on the Danube and the Lech were, during Gustavus Adolphus's progress to Saxony, defended by Count Birkenfeld, and the Swedish general Bannier, against the Bavarians. But too weak to oppose the bravery
of

of the latter, which was fuſtained by the experience of the Imperial general Altringer, they were under the neceſſity of calling the Swediſh general, Guſtavus Horn, from Alſace. After that experienced hero had ſubjected the towns of Benfeld, Schlettſtadt, Colmar, and Hagenau, to the Swediſh arms, he left their defence to the Rhingrave Otto Louis, and haſtened over the Rhine to form a junction with Bannier's army. But, although it conſiſted of 16,000 men, it could not prevent the enemy from taking an advantageous poſition on the borders of Suabia, gaining Kempten, and being joined by ſeven regiments from Bohemia. In order to protect the important banks of the Lech and **the** Danube, the Rhingrave Otto Louis was called from Alſace, where he could ſcarce defend himſelf againſt the exaſperated peaſantry. He was obliged to reinforce the army of the Danube; and as this ſuccour was yet inſufficient, Duke Bernard of Weimar **was** called to that quarter.

That general had, ſoon after the opening of the campaign in 1633, taken poſſeſſion of the city and biſhopric of Bamberg, and threatened Wirtzburg with the ſame fate. Upon the invitation of Guſtavus Horn, he immediately
began

began his march towards the Danube, beat a Bavarian army under John de Werth on his way, and joined the Swedes near Donauwerth. These numerous armies, commanded by excellent generals, threatened Bavaria with a terrible inroad. The entire bishopric of Eichstadt was overrun, and Ingolstadt was ready to fall into the Swedish hands by treachery. Altringer's activity was restrained by the express orders of Wallenstein; and left without assistance from Bohemia, he could not oppose the enemy's progress. The most favourable circumstances combined to promote the fortune of the Swedish arms in this quarter, when all on a sudden the army was stopped by a quarrel among the officers.

Every thing had hitherto been acquired in Germany by arms; even Gustavus Adolphus owed his greatness to the discipline of his army, their bravery and persevering courage amidst every danger and difficulty. However wisely his plans were formed in the cabinet, it was by the army they were executed; and the extended views of the leader continually imposed new burdens upon the troops. All the decisive advantages in this war were obtained by a barbarous sacrifice of the soldiers lives in winter campaigns,

campaigns, forced marches, storms, and pitched battles; and it was Gustavus Adolphus's maxim never to decline a victory, provided it cost no more than men. The soldiers became sensible of their importance, and naturally required a share of the booty which was purchased at their expense: but instead of this they hardly received their pay; and the avarice of their leaders or the necessities of the state generally consumed the best part of the money which was raised either in contributions or in the conquered states. The soldier had no other prospect for all his toils but the doubtful chance of plunder or promotion, in both of which he was often disappointed. Fear and hope had indeed suppressed every open complaint during the life of Gustavus Adolphus; but after his death the murmurs were loud and universal, and the soldier seized the most dangerous moment to remind his superiors of his importance. Two officers, Pfuhl and Mitschefal, who had, during the King's life, been considered as restless characters, afforded, at the camp upon the Danube, an example which was soon after followed by all the officers of the army. They agreed among themselves not to obey any order until they had received their arrears which were due for a considerable time, and also a present prefent to each in either money or land according to his fervices. "Immenfe fums," faid they, "were daily raifed in contributions, and "all this was kept in a few hands. They "were obliged to ferve in the fevereft weather "without being rewarded for their inceffant "toil. The foldiers are blamed at Hailbron, "but nobody talks of rewarding them. The "whole world refounds with the noife of bat- "tles and fieges, but thefe victories are all "their work."

The number of the malcontents increafed, and they even invited the armies on the Rhine and in Saxony to follow their example, by letters which were fortunately intercepted. Neither the reprefentations of the Duke of Weimar, nor the reproaches of his feverer affociates, could fuppress this mutiny, which difcipline feemed to increafe. They required that each regiment fhould receive a number of cities, that they might obtain payment of their arrears. Four weeks were given to the Chancellor to confider their demands, and in cafe of refufal, they declared that they would pay themfelves, and never more draw a fword for Sweden.

This

This bold demand was made at the very time that the military chest was exhausted, and credit at a low ebb; and it was necessary speedily to remedy it before the contagion spread among the rest of the troops. Among all the Swedish generals there was only one who had influence and consideration among the soldiers to terminate this quarrel. The Duke of Weimar was the favourite of the army, and his prudent moderation gained him the attachment of the troops, while his military experience excited their admiration. He now undertook to quell the mutiny; but feeling his importance, he seized the favourable moment of first stipulating for himself, and turning the Swedish Chancellor's embarrassment to his own advantage.

Gustavus Adolphus had already flattered him with hopes of the dutchy of Franconia, which was to be formed from the bishoprics of Bamberg and Wirtzburg; and he now insisted upon the performance of this promise. He at the same time required the chief command of the army, as Swedish generalissimo. This abuse which the Duke made of his influence so exasperated Oxenstern, that on the first moment he offered to dismiss him the Swedish service. But

But he soon after thought better of it, and, instead of sacrificing so important a general, to attach him by any price to the Swedish interest. He immediately gave him up the Franconian bishoprics, together with two fortresses of Wirtzberg and Koenigshofen, as an investiture of the Swedish crown, and at the same time engaged to maintain him in the possession. The command which he required was refused under a specious pretext. The Duke did not long delay to display his gratitude; and by his influence and activity, tranquillity was soon restored to the army. Great sums of money were divided among the officers, together with large estates, whose value amounted to 5,000,000 of dollars, and to which they had no other claim than the right of conquest. In the mean time the opportunity was lost for a great undertaking, and the united generals now separated to oppose the enemy in another quarter.

After Gustavus Horn had made a short inroad into the Upper Palatinate, he directed his march towards the borders of Suabia, where the Imperialists had considerably reinforced themselves, and threatened to ravage Wirtemberg. But terrified by his approach, the enemy retired to the lake of Bode, only to bring the Swedes

Swedes after them. A possession on the entrance of Switzerland was desirable, and the town of Costnitz seemed peculiarly fitted to introduce him to the alliance of the cantons. Horn immediately undertook to besiege it; but not having sufficient artillery, which he was obliged to transport from Wirtemberg, he could not prosecute the undertaking with so much vigour as to prevent the enemy from throwing a sufficient reinforcement into the place, which was easily effected upon the lake. He accordingly raised the siege after an ineffectual attempt, and directed his attention to a pressing danger upon the Danube.

At the Emperor's instigation, the Cardinal Infant, brother to Philip IV. King of Spain, and viceroy of Milan, raised an army of 14,000 men, which was destined, independent of Wallenstein, to act upon the Rhine and defend Alsace. This army now appeared in Bavaria under the command of the Duke of Feria, a Spaniard; and that they might be used immediately against the Swedes, Altringer was ordered to join them. Upon the first intelligence of their approach, Horn had recalled the Count Palatine of Birkenfeld from the Rhine to his assistance; and, after he had joined

joined him at Stockach, advanced boldly upon an army of 30,000 men which the enemy had collected. The latter had marched over the Danube towards Suabia, where Horn at one time was so near them that both armies were only half a mile from each other. But instead of accepting the offer of a battle, the Imperialists retired over the Black Forest towards Brisgau and Alsace, where they arrived in sufficient time to relieve Brisach, and to stop the victorious career of the Rhingrave Otto Louis. This general had a short time before taken the Forest cities, and, supported by the Palatine of Birkenfeld, who delivered the Lower Palatinate, and beat the Duke of Lorrain, had obtained the Swedish arms once more the superiority in that quarter. But now he was obliged to yield to the powerful numbers of the enemy. Horn and Birkenfeld, however, soon came to his assistance, and the Imperialists, after a short triumph, were driven out of **Alsace**. The severity of the autumn destroyed most of the Italians on their retreat, and the general himself, the Duke of Feria, died of a broken heart.

Meanwhile the Duke of Weimar had taken up his position on the Danube, with eighteen regiments

regiments of foot and 140 squadrons of horse, both to cover Franconia and watch the motions of the Imperial-Bavarian army upon that river. No sooner had Altringer withdrawn his troops to join the Italians than the Duke profited by his absence, crossed the Danube, and immediately appeared before Ratisbon. The possession of this city decided the undertaking of the Swedes in Bavaria and Austria; it obtained them a firm footing on the Danube, secured them a retreat in case of misfortune, and it was by its possession only that they could expect to make a durable conquest in the country. Tilly's dying advice was, to defend Ratisbon; and Gustavus Adolphus lamented it as an irreparable loss that the Bavarians had been beforehand with him in taking possession of this place. Maximilian's consternation was excessive when Duke Bernard appeared before the city, and prepared to besiege it.

The garrison consisted only of fifteen companies of foot, yet that was a sufficient number to delay the enemy, if supported by faithful and warlike inhabitants. But this was the very enemy which the Bavarian garrison had most reason to fear. The Protestant inhabitants of Ratisbon, equally jealous of their civil and religious

ligious rights, had submitted to the Bavarian yoke with impatience, and long wished to be delivered from it. The Duke's arrival before their walls filled them with the sincerest joy, and it was to be dreaded that they would support the besiegers by an interior tumult. In this embarrassment the Elector made the most pressing instances to the Emperor and Wallenstein to assist him with even 5000 men. Seven messengers successively were sent by Ferdinand, with this order, to Wallenstein, who promised immediate assistance, and even announced to the Elector the near approach of 12,000 men, commanded by Gallas, but forbad that general, under pain of death, to hasten. The Bavarian governor of Ratisbon, in the hope of speedy relief, took the best measures of defence. The Catholic peasantry were armed, the Protestant inhabitants disarmed and closely watched, lest they should execute some hostile design against the garrison. But as no relief appeared, and the enemy's artillery incessantly cannonaded the walls, he consulted his own safety and that of his garrison by a favourable capitulation, and abandoned the Bavarians and the clergy to the conqueror's mercy.

With

With the possession of Ratisbon the Duke's projects expanded, and reached beyond Bavaria itself. He intended penetrating as far as Austria, arming the Protestant inhabitants against the Emperor, and to restore them to their liberty of conscience. He had already taken Straubingen, while another Swedish general subdued the north bank of the Danube. At the head of his Swedes, bidding defiance to the severity of the weather, he reached the mouth of the river Iser, which he passed in the presence of the Bavarian general Werth, who was here encamped. Passau and Lintznow trembled, and the embarrassed Emperor redoubled his orders to Wallenstein to hasten to the assistance of Bavaria. But here the Duke of Weimar's progress was stopped : having the river Inn in front, which was defended by a number of strong castles, and behind, two enemy's armies; being in a disaffected country, where no tenable position covered his rear, and the frost permitted no intrenchments, and threatened by the entire army of Wallenstein, which had at length begun to approach the Danube, he made a timely retreat, to avoid the danger of being cut off from Ratisbon, and surrounded by the enemy. He hastened over the Iser and the Danube to maintain the conquests

quests in the Upper Palatinate, and even, if neceſſary, to give the Imperialiſts battle. But Wallenſtein, who had never intended to perform great exploits upon the Danube, did not await his approach, and before the Bavarians could well expreſs their joy, he had returned into Bohemia. The Duke thus ended his glorious campaign, and granted his troops their well-earned repoſe in winter-quarters upon an enemy's country.

While the war was maintained with ſuch ſuperiority in Suabia by Guſtavus Horn, the Palatine Birkenfeld, General Baudiſſin, and the Rhingrave Otto Louis, upon the Upper and Lower Rhine, and by the Duke of Weimar upon the Danube, the reputation of the Swediſh arms was ſuſtained in Lower Saxony and Weſtphalia by the Duke of Lunenburg and the Landgrave of Heſſe Caſſel with equal glory. The former took the fortreſs of Hameln after the braveſt reſiſtance, and the united Swediſh and Heſſian army obtained a brilliant victory at Oldendorf over the Imperial General Gromsfeld. Count Waſaburg, a natural ſon of Guſtavus Adolphus, ſhowed in this battle that he was worthy of his extraction; ſixteen cannon, the whole baggage of the Imperialiſts, together with

with seventy-four colours, fell into the Swedish hands; about 3000 of the enemy remained dead on the spot, and almost an equal number was taken prisoners; the town of Ofnaburg submitted to the Swedish Colonel Knyphaufen, and Paderborn to the Landgrave of Hesse Cassel; but on the other hand Buckeburg, a very important place for the Swedes, was gained by the Imperialists. The Swedish arms were seen victorious in almost all quarters of Germany, and the year after Gustavus Adolphus's death showed no marks of the loss which had been sustained in the person of that great hero.

By a review of the important circumstances which distinguished the campaign of 1633, we are justly astonished at the inactivity of a man from whom the greatest expectations were formed. Of all the generals who distinguished themselves in this campaign, there was none who could be compared with Wallenstein in experience, talents, or reputation, and yet he immediately disappeared after the battle of Lutzen; the death of his great antagonist now left him master of the theatre, and all Europe expected from him exploits which should efface the memory of his defeat, and display his skill

in

in the art of war. Nevertheless he remained inactive in Bohemia, while the Emperor's losses in Bavaria, Lower Saxony, and the Rhine, loudly called for his assistance; a behaviour unintelligible both to friends and enemies, while he was the terror, and at the same time the Emperor's last hope. He had withdrawn into Bohemia with unaccountable rapidity after his defeat at Lutzen, and instituted the severest inquiry into the conduct of his officers in that battle; such as the council of war declared guilty were **executed** without pity, those who had behaved with bravery were princely rewarded, and the memory of the deceased was eternized by splendid monuments: he oppressed the Imperial provinces with immoderate contributions and by winter-quarters, which he purposely did not take up in an enemy's country, that he might exhaust the Austrian territories. Instead of being the first to open the campaign at the head of his formidable army in the spring of 1633, and displaying his great abilities, he was the last that appeared in the field, and it **was** then an hereditary province of Austria **which** he made the theatre of war.

Of all the possessions of Austria, Silesia was exposed to the greatest danger. Three different
armies,

armies, a Swedish under Count Thurn, a Saxon
under Arnheim and the Duke of Lauenburg,
together with one of Brandenburg under Burgs-
dorf, had at the same time carried the war into
that country; they had already taken possession
of the most important places, and even Breslau
embraced the party of the allies. But it was
this number of generals and armies which saved
the country; for the jealousy of the commanders, and the mutual hatred of the Swedes
and Saxons, did not permit them to act with
union. Arnheim and Thurn quarrelled for the
supreme command; the Brandenburgers and
Saxons detested the Swedes, whom they looked
upon as troublesome strangers, and who were
to be got rid of as soon as possible; the Saxons,
on the contrary, lived upon a very intimate
footing with the Austrians, and the officers of
both armies often visited and entertained each
other; the Imperialists were openly permitted
to remove their effects, and many did not conceal their having remitted large sums to Vienna.
Among such allies the Swedes were sold and
betrayed, and with such a bad understanding
no design of importance could be executed;
General Arnheim was also frequently absent,
and when he returned to the army Wallenstein
appeared

appeared with a formidable force upon the frontiers.

He was at the head of 40,000 men, when the allies had only 24,000 to oppose him; they, nevertheless, resolved to give him battle, and advanced to Munsterberg, where he had intrenched himself. But Wallenstein remained motionless during eight days; he then forsook his intrenchments, and slowly advanced against the enemy; but though the latter did not decline meeting him, he neglected the opportunity of engaging. The care with which he, upon this occasion, avoided a battle, was represented as the effects of fear, but the established reputation of Wallenstein might brave such a suspicion; the vanity of the allies did not let them perceive that he was engaged in the same cause with themselves, and that he magnanimously saved them defeats, merely because a victory over them would now be of no service to him. But in order to convince them that his inaction did not proceed from a fear of their resentment, he put to death the commander of a castle who fell into his hands, for having dared to resist in an untenable place.

Both

Both armies remained at the distance of a musket-shot during nine days, when Count Terzky appeared before the allied camp, accompanied by a trumpeter from Wallenstein, and invited General Arnheim to a conference. The purpose of this was, notwithstanding Wallenstein's superiority, to request a cessation of arms for six weeks. "He was come," he said, " to conclude a lasting peace with the Swedes " and the princes of the Empire; to pay the " troops, and obtain satisfaction for every indi- " vidual; every thing lay in his power, and " if his measures were delayed to be confirmed, " he would join the allies, and (as he privately " intimated to Arnheim) depose the Emperor." At a second parley he explained himself more fully to Count Thurn. "All the Bohemian " privileges," he declared, " should be con- " firmed, the exiles recalled and reinstated in " their properties, and he would himself be " the first to restore his share of the confisca- " tions; the Jesuits should be banished as the " authors of all the disturbances and oppres- " sions; the crown of Sweden should be in- " demnified its expenses, and all the troops " which could be spared upon both sides should " be led against the Turks." The last condition explained the whole mystery: "That
" if

"if he should obtain the crown of Bohemia, the
"exiles would have cause to applaud his
"generosity; perfect toleration of religion
"should prevail in the kingdom; the Palatine
"family should be restored to its rights; and
"he would content himself with Moravia as a
"compensation for the loss of Mecklenburg.
"The allied army should then march to Vienna,
"and compel the Emperor to confirm these
"conditions."

The plan which had occupied him for years, and was concealed by the most impenetrable silence, was now at once discovered; every circumstance also taught him that no time was to be lost in its execution. It was only that blind confidence in the good fortune and superior genius of Wallenstein which could fascinate the Emperor, and led him, contrary to the remonstrances of Spain and Bavaria, as well as at the expense of his own power, to confer upon this imperious man such an unlimited command. But this belief of Wallenstein's being invincible, was much weakened by his long inactivity, and at last almost totally destroyed by the defeat at Lutzen; his enemies renewed their intrigues against him at the Imperial court, and the Emperor's disappointment and

and difcontent obtained their remonftrances a more favourable reception with that monarch. Wallenftein's whole conduct was now reviewed with a malicious criticifm; his dangerous haughtinefs, and his difobedience to the Emperor's orders, were brought to that jealous prince's remembrance; recourfe was had to the complaints of the Auftrian fubjects of his infupportable oppreffion; his fidelity **was** rendered fufpicious, and dangerous hints were thrown out of his private defigns. Thefe complaints, which were fupported by the General's conduct, did not fail to make a deep impreffion upon Ferdinand; but the ftep had been taken, and the great power which was conferred on Wallenftein, he could not be deprived of without danger: gradually to diminifh it, was all that remained for the Emperor, and to do this with effect, it muft, above all things, be divided, and the dependance upon the General's attachment muft be removed; this power had, however, been conferred in the agreement which had been made with him, and the Emperor's own fignature fecured him the abfolute command of the troops. As this pernicious agreement could neither be broken nor obferved, recourfe was had to ftratagem. Wallenftein was the Imperial generaliffimo in Germany, but his authority

rity extended no further, and over a foreign force he could exercise no authority; a Spanish army was accordingly raised in Milan, and under a Spanish general introduced into Germany. Wallenstein now ceased to be longer indispensable because he had been unfortunate, and there was not wanting a support against him in case of necessity.

Wallenstein instantly perceived whence proceeded the blow, and where it was directed. In vain did he protest against this innovation with the Cardinal Infant; the Spanish army advanced, and he was compelled to detach General Altringer with a reinforcement to join it. He was, indeed, by his injunctions, so well able to restrain the latter, that the Italian army acquired no reputation in Alsace and in Suabia; but this powerful measure of the Court had aroused him from his security, and warned him against the approach of danger. To avoid being a second time deprived of his command, and losing the fruits of all his labours, he must hasten to execute his design; he secured the attachment of his troops by removing the suspicious officers, and by his munificence to the rest; to the welfare of the army he had sacrificed every other order in the state, and all
consider-

considerations of justice and humanity; and he accordingly expected its ready acquiescence in return. On the point of exhibiting an unparalleled instance of ingratitude against the author of his good fortune, he founded all his own hopes upon the gratitude which was to be shown to himself.

The leaders of the Silesian armies had no authority to conclude a peace with Wallenstein, and even the cessation of hostilities they would agree to only for a fortnight. Before Wallenstein had disclosed his secret to the Swedes and Saxons, he had the precaution to secure himself the protection of France in his new undertaking; for this purpose a private negotiation was carried on by means of Count Kinsky, with the French ambassador Feuquieres in Dresden, but with extreme caution; and it terminated entirely to his advantage. Feuquieres received orders from his court to promise Wallenstein every assistance on the part of France, and to offer him, in case of need, a considerable pecuniary aid.

But it was this excessive caution to secure himself on all sides which led him to ruin. The French ambassador with astonishment discovered

covered that a plan, which above all others should be kept secret, had been communicated to the Swedes and Saxons; the Saxon ministry was well known to be in the Emperor's interests, and the conditions offered to the Swedes fell too short of their expectations to be accepted. Feuquieres, therefore, found it inconceivable how **Wallenstein could in** earnest depend upon the support of the former, or the discretion of the latter; he communicated his cares and doubts to the Swedish Chancellor, who was equally distrustful of Wallenstein's designs, and by no means relished his offers. Although it was no secret to him that Wallenstein had formerly entered into a similar negotiation with Gustavus Adolphus, yet he could not conceive the possibility of bringing a whole army to revolt, or of executing his extravagant projects; such an immense design, and such imprudent conduct, seemed but ill to agree with the dark suspicious character of Wallenstein, and it was the rather attributed to deceit, as his sincerity was more doubtful than his prudence. Oxenstern's doubts were at length communicated to Arnheim, who, confident of Wallenstein's sincerity, had repaired to the Chancellor at Gelhausen, in order to ask his permission to lend some of his best regiments for the execution of the

the plan: they began to suspect that this offer was only a snare to disarm the allies, and betray the flower of their troops into the Emperor's hands. Wallenstein's notorious character sanctioned this bad suspicion, and the contradictions in which he afterwards involved himself entirely deceived them. While he courted the alliance of Oxenstern, and even demanded his best troops, he declared to Arnheim that he must begin by expelling the Swedes from Germany; and while the Saxon officers, confident of the sincerity of the truce, repaired in great numbers to his camp, he made an unsuccessful attempt to seize upon them. He first broke the cessation of arms, which he with much difficulty renewed several months afterwards; all confidence was lost in his sincerity, and his whole conduct was regarded as the offspring of treachery and low cunning, with a view to weaken the allies and recover himself; but this he actually effected, while he daily augmented his army, and the allies lost half their troops by bad management and desertion. But he did not profit of his superiority as was expected in Vienna; when an important event was near, he on a sudden renewed the negotiation; and when the truce lulled the allies into security, he as suddenly commenced hostilities. All these contra-

contradictions proceeded from the double and opposite designs of ruining the Emperor and the Swedes at the same time, and concluding a separate peace with the Saxons.

Rendered impatient by the ill success of his negotiation, he at length determined to display his strength; besides that the necessities of the Empire and the increasing displeasure of the Imperial court did not admit any further delay. Before the last cessation of arms, General Holk fell from Bohemia into the circle of Meissen, ravaged the country with fire and sword, drove the Elector to his fortresses, and took Leipzig. But the truce in Silesia put a period to his successes, and the consequences of his intemperance brought him at Adorf to the grave. After the recommencement of hostilities, Wallenstein made a movement as if he designed to penetrate through Lusatia into Saxony, and spread a report that Piccolomini was already marched towards that quarter; Arnheim immediately broke up his camp to follow him and succour the Electorate; by this he exposed the Swedes, who were encamped in small numbers at Steinau on the Oder, and this was exactly what Wallenstein desired. He permitted the Saxon general to hasten before him sixteen miles

miles towards Meiffen, and on a fudden returned to the Oder, where he furprifed the Swedes in the utmoft fecurity; their cavalry were firft beaten by General Schafgotfch, and their infantry was fully furrounded by Wallenftein's army which followed. Wallenftein gave Count Thurn half an hour to confider whether he fhould defend himfelf with 2500 men againft more than 20,000, or furrender at difcretion; but no alternative could find a place in fuch a fituation; the whole corps furrendered, and the completeft victory was obtained without bloodfhed: colours, baggage, and artillery, all fell into the conqueror's hands: the officers were taken into cuftody, and the private men compelled to ferve. After a fourteen years banifhment and numberlefs reverfes of fortune, the author of the Bohemian infurrection and of this deftructive war, the famous Count Thurn, was in the hands of his enemies. With a bloodthirfty impatience the arrival of this great criminal was awaited in Vienna, where the terrible triumph of facrificing fo diftinguifhed a victim to public juftice was already anticipated. But depriving the Jefuits of that pleafure was a more agreeable triumph, and Thurn obtained his liberty; fortunately for him, he knew more than was prudent to divulge in Vienna, and

Wallen-

Wallenstein's enemies were also *his*; a defeat would sooner have been forgiven at Vienna than this disappointed hope. " What could I " have done with that madman?" said Wallenstein to those who called him to account for this ill-timed magnanimity; " would to hea-
" ven," added he, " the enemy's generals were
" all such as Thurn! at the head of the
" Swedish army he will render us much better
" service than in prison."

The victory at Steinau was followed by the taking of Leignitz, Gross-Glogau, and even Frankfort on the Oder. Schafgotsch, who remained in Silesia to complete the subjection of that province, blockaded Brieg and threatened Breslau, but in vain, as that free city was jealous of its privileges, and devoted to the Swedes. Wallenstein detached Colonels Illo and Goetz to the Warta, in order to penetrate through Pomerania as far as the coasts of the Baltic; and Landsberg, the key of Pomerania, was actually taken by them. While he made the Elector of Brandenburg and the Duke of Pomerania tremble for their dominions, Wallenstein with the rest of his army entered Lusatia, where he took Goerlitz by storm, and compelled Bautzen to surrender: but his intention

tion was to terrify the Elector of Saxony not to prosecute the advantages he had obtained. He also, with the sword in his hand, offered to treat with Brandenburg and Saxony, but without success, his repeated contradictions having destroyed all confidence in him. He would now have turned his arms against the unfortunate Saxony, and have pursued his projects by force, if circumstances had not compelled him to abandon that country. The Duke of Weimar's victory on the Danube, which threatened Austria itself with danger, immediately required his presence in Bavaria; and the expulsion of the Swedes and Saxons from Silesia left him no further pretext for disobeying the Emperor's commands, and leaving the Elector of Bavaria at the enemy's mercy. He accordingly advanced against the Upper Palatinate, and his retreat freed Saxony for ever from this formidable enemy.

Wallenstein had delayed saving Bavaria as long as possible, and evaded the Emperor's orders under various pretexts. After repeated entreaties he detached to Count Altringer, who endeavoured to maintain the Lech and the Danube against the Duke of Weimar and Horn, some regiments from Bohemia, but with express orders

orders to act defensively. Whenever the Emperor or the Elector required assistance he referred them to Altringer, who, he said, had full powers of acting: but he privately tied this general by the severest instructions, and even threatened him with death if he should exceed his orders. After the Duke of Weimar was advanced before Ratisbon, and the Emperor as well as the Elector renewed their demands of aid, he pretended to send General Gallas with a considerable army to the Danube; but this was not executed, and the Swedes took the bishopric of Eichstadt, together with Ratisbon, Straubingen, and Cham. When he could at length oppose the orders of the court no longer, he moved slowly towards the frontiers of Bavaria, where he recovered Cham from the Swedes. But he no sooner learned that the Swedes were preparing to make a diversion, by means of an inroad of the Saxons into Bohemia, than he immediately took advantage of that pretext to march, without giving the least notice, into that kingdom. Every consideration, he said, must be postponed to the defence of the hereditary dominions; and thus he remained firm in Bohemia, which he defended as if his own property. The Emperor reiterated his orders to him for proceeding towards
the

the Danube, and preventing the Duke of Weimar from occupying a position upon the frontiers of Auftria. He, however, ended the campaign for this year, and again took up his winter-quarters in that exhaufted kingdom.

Such a continued infolence, fo unexampled a contempt of the Imperial orders, and fo vifible a neglect of the common caufe, joined with fuch an equivocal behaviour towards the enemy, muft have at length excited the Emperor's belief of the unfavourable reports which were fpread throughout Germany. Wallenftein had for a long time fucceeded in juftifying his criminal correfpondence with the enemy, under the colour of moderation, and perfuaded his indulgent monarch that the end of his private interviews was to obtain a peace for Germany. But however fecret he thought his defigns, the whole of his conduct juftified the accufations with which his enemies perpetually affailed the Emperor's ears. In order to obtain certain information concerning this affair, the Emperor had already, at different times, fent fpies into Wallenftein's camp; but as the latter had the precaution to commit nothing to writing, they returned only with conjectures. But at length the minifters themfelves, who had hitherto defended

fended him, upon their estates being equally oppressed with the rest, joined his enemies; and the Elector of Bavaria threatened, that if he was employed any longer, he would himself join the Swedes. The Spanish ambassador also insisted upon his dismissal, and threatened, in case of refusal, to withdraw the subsidies of his crown: and Ferdinand at length found himself obliged to deprive Wallenstein a second time of the command. The Emperor's positive orders soon taught Wallenstein that his agreement with the former was broken, and his dismissal inevitable. One of his inferior generals in Austria, whom he had forbidden, under pain of death, to obey the court, received the Emperor's immediate command to join the Elector of Bavaria; and Wallenstein himself was expressly ordered to send some regiments to join the Cardinal Infant, who was marching with his army from Italy. All these measures convinced him that the design was formed to disarm him by degrees, and then to precipitate him into ruin.

He must now hasten the execution of a plan in self-defence which was originally formed for his aggrandizement. He had delayed it too long, either because the favourable constellations were wanting, or, as he used to answer

to the impatience of his friends, " the favour-
" able moment was not yet arrived :" but neceffity no longer gave time to wait for the
friendly ftars. His firft ftep was to try the
fentiments of the principal officers, and then
experience the attachment of the army, of
which he had fo long been confident. Three
colonels, Kinfky, Terfky, and Illo, had long
known the fecret, and the two firft were allied
to him. An equal ambition, an equal hatred
to government, and the hopes of an immenfe
recompence, clofely united them with Wallenftein, who ftooped to the loweft means to increafe the number of his dependants. He had
once advifed Colonel Illo to folicit the title of
Count in Vienna, and promifed to fupport his
application. But he at the fame time wrote
privately to the minifter to refufe the requeft,
becaufe a number of others who had equal merit
might make fimilar applications. On Illo's
return to the camp his firft queftion to him
was concerning his fuccefs : and when the latter
had informed him of his failure, he broke out
into the fevereft complaints againft the court.
" Our faithful fervices, then, are thus re-
" warded!" cried he. " My recommendations
" are neglected, and your merit denied fo
" fmall a reward ! Who will devote his fer-
" vices

"vices to such an ungrateful master any
"longer? No; for my part, I am hence-
"forward the determined enemy of the House
"of Austria." Illo coincided with him, and
a close connexion was formed between them.

But what was known to those three confi-
dants was long an impenetrable secret to the
remainder, and the confidence with which
Wallenstein spoke of the attachment of his officers was merely founded upon his generosity
to them, and upon their discontent with the
court. But he must convert these doubtful
surmises into certainty before he could venture
to throw off the mask, and openly oppose the
Emperor. Count Piccolomini, who had distinguished himself at the battle of Lutzen by
an unexampled intrepidity, was the first on
whose fidelity he tried the experiment. He
had attached to himself this general by great
gifts, and preferred him before all others because born under the same constellations. He
declared to him that, exasperated by Ferdinand's ingratitude, and alarmed by the near
approach of danger, he was determined entirely
to abandon the Emperor's cause, to join the
enemy with the best part of the army, and
attack

attack the House of Austria in all quarters. He had principally depended upon Piccolomini, and promised him previously the greatest rewards. When the latter had expressed his astonishment at this sudden and surprising offer, and spoke of the obstacles and dangers with which the design was attended, Wallenstein turned his fears into ridicule.

"Such enterprises," said he, "were only
"difficult at the commencement; the stars
"were propitious to him, the opportunity was
"the best which could be wished, and some-
"thing must be trusted to fortune. His re-
"solution was fixed, and if it could not be
"otherwise, he would venture upon his scheme
"at the head of a thousand horse." Piccolomini was cautious not to excite Wallenstein's suspicion by contradiction, and pretended to yield to the weight of his arguments. Such was Wallenstein's infatuation, that, notwithstanding the warning of Colonel Terfky, he did not doubt the sincerity of the man, who lost not a moment to have this important discovery communicated to the Court of Vienna.

In order to take the last and most important step, he called a meeting of all the commanders

manders of the army, in January 1634, at Pilsen, whither he had marched after his retreat from Bavaria. The Emperor's new directions, no longer to take up winter-quarters in the hereditary states, to recover Ratisbon in the middle of winter, and to take 6000 cavalry from the army in order to reinforce the Cardinal Infant, were points of sufficient importance for the discussion of a council of war; and under colour of this pretext Wallenstein concealed the true purpose of the meeting. Sweden and Saxony were even invited to it, in order privately to conclude a treaty with Wallenstein; and a correspondence was to be commenced with the distant armies. Twenty of the commanders who were cited appeared; but three of the principal ones, Gallas, Colloredo, and Altringer, were absent. Wallenstein repeated his citations to them; but expecting their speedy arrival, he in the mean time proceeded to execute his designs.

He was now entered upon an undertaking of no small difficulty. To declare a nobility, proved brave and jealous of its honour, capable of the most infamous treachery, was making them appear, in the eyes of those who were ever accustomed to consider them as the support

port of monarchy, the judges of honour, and the guardians of the laws, to be now rebels and traitors. It was not less difficult to shake to its foundation a power rendered sacred by years, constitution, and religion; to dissolve the enchantment of the senses and the imagination, the formidable guardians of a legal throne; and to annihilate by force that invincible sense of duty which every subject feels towards his native sovereign. But, blinded by the splendour of a crown, Wallenstein never considered the abyss which he was opening for himself; and full of reliance on his own strength, the common fate of great minds, he imagined that he would be able to surmount every obstacle. Wallenstein could see nothing but an army partly indifferent and partly exasperated against the court—an army which was accustomed to follow him with blind obedience, and to receive with awful respect his commands, as the decrees of fate. By the excessive flatteries he received, by the bold calumnies against court and government which an unlicensed soldiery indulged itself in, and which the freedom of the camp permitted, he thought he had learned the true sentiments of the army; and the boldness with which the monarch's measures were criticised, guaranteed to him its attachment upon renouncing his allegiance to so contemptible a sovereign. But what he thought so easily overcome was his most formidable obstacle; all his hopes failed before the sense which the troops retained of their allegiance. Deceived by the profound respect in which he was held, he put every dependance upon his personal greatness, without making a proper difference between himself and the dignity of the station which he filled. Every thing trembled before him while he exercised a lawful authority, while obedience to him was duty, and while his consequence was supported by the majesty of the sovereign. **His** own greatness could raise terror and admiration, but legal greatness could alone excite respect and obedience. And of this decisive advantage he was deprived the moment he unmasked himself as a traitor. All the bonds of fidelity were destroyed between him and his army so soon as he dissolved the more sacred one which bound him to the throne, and his violation of duty was retorted upon him in the influence which he had obtained among his troops.

Illo undertook to learn the sentiments of the commanders, and prepare them for the step which was meditating. He began with stating the new demands of the court to the general and the army; and by the obnoxious turn which

which he gave them it was eafy to inflame the indignation of the whole affembly. After this well-chofen preface he expatiated with much eloquence upon the merits of the army, and of its general, and upon the ingratitude with which the Emperor intended to requite them. " Spanifh influence," he faid, " directed every meafure of the court: Wal-
" lenftein alone had hitherto refifted this ty-
" ranny, and therefore expofed himfelf to the
" mortal hatred of the Spaniards. To remove
" him from the army, or to accomplifh his
" death, was," added he, " long the end of
" their defires; and until they fhould effect
" the one or the other they endeavoured to
" abridge his power in the field. The com-
" mand was to be given to the King of Hun-
" gary, for no other reafon than that this
" prince, as the ready inftrument of foreign
" councils, might be led at pleafure, the better
" to promote the Spanifh power in Germany.
" It was merely to weaken the army that 6000
" men were required for the Cardinal Infant;
" it **was** entirely to deftroy them that they were
" required in the middle of winter to lay fiege
" to Ratifbon. Every means of fubfifting the
" army was rendered difficult, while the Jefuits
" and the minifters enriched themfelves with

" the

"the treasures of the provinces, and squan-
"dered the money which was intended for the
"troops. The general, abandoned by the
"court, acknowledged his inability to perform
"his promise with the army. For all the ser-
"vices which he had, during twenty-two
"years, rendered the House of Austria, for all
"the pains which he had taken, and for all the
"riches which he had expended of his own
"property to promote the Imperial service, a
"second disgraceful resignation was now re-
"quired of him: but he declared that he
"never would consent to that. He would of
"his own accord give up the command rather
"than be forcibly deprived of it. This," continued the speaker, " is what he has commis-
"sioned me to say. Let every one now ask
"himself if it will be prudent to lose such a
"general. Let each consider who will refund
"him the sums which he has expended in the
"Emperor's service, and where he can obtain
"the reward of his valour, when he, before
"whom it was exerted, is no more."

A general cry that they would not abandon
their commander interrupted the speaker. Four
of the principals were deputed to lay before
him the desires of the meeting, and earnestly

to requeſt he would not leave the army. Wallenſtein made an appearance of reſiſtance, and only yielded after a ſecond deputation. This condeſcenſion upon his ſide ſeemed to deſerve a return upon theirs. As he engaged not to quit the ſervice without the knowledge and conſent of the generals, he required from them a written promiſe to be faithful to him, never to permit a ſeparation, and to defend him to the laſt drop of their blood. Whoever refuſed to ſign this engagement was to be conſidered as a traitor, and treated by the remainder as a common enemy. The expreſs condition which was added, " *So long as Wal-* " *lenſtein ſhall continue to uſe the army for the* " *Emperor's ſervice,*" ſeemed to exclude every miſtake, and none of the generals heſitated to grant a requeſt ſo apparently innocent and reaſonable.

This paper was publicly read before an entertainment which Field-marſhal Illo had ordered for the purpoſe; and it was intended to be ſigned on riſing from table. The hoſt did his utmoſt to intoxicate his gueſts; and it was not until he had effected his purpoſe that he produced the paper for ſignature. Moſt of them wrote their names, without knowing what they

they signed; only a few, more curious than the rest, threw their eyes over it a second time, and to their astonishment discovered that the clause, *" So long as Wallenstein shall use the army for " the Emperor's service,"* was omitted. Illo had artfully substituted a second copy for the first, and left out the above clause. The deceit was open, and many now refused to sign their names. Piccolomini, who saw through the whole cheat, and who only assisted at this meeting to inform the court of its proceedings, forgot himself so much in his cups as to drink the Emperor's health. But Count Tersky now rose, and declared all were perjured villains who should recede from their promise. His threats, and the idea of the inevitable danger to which those who resisted any longer should be exposed, the example of the majority, and Illo's oratory, at length overcame every scruple, and the paper was signed without exception.

Wallenstein had now effected his purpose, but the unexpected resistance of the generals at once aroused him from the favourite presumption in which he had indulged himself; besides this, most of the names were so illegibly scrawled, that dishonest intentions were manifest. But instead of taking this serious warning

into

into confideration, his pride broke out in loud complaints and reproaches; he affembled the generals the next morning, and renewed the bufinefs of the foregoing day; after he had exhaufted himfelf in the fevereft reproaches againft the court, he remarked upon their refiftance, and declared that this circumftance would induce him to retract his promife. The generals filently withdrew, and after a fhort confultation in the antechamber, returned to excufe themfelves for their late behaviour, and offered to fign the paper anew.

Nothing now remained but to obtain a fimilar affurance from the abfent generals, or, on their refufal, to feize their perfons. Wallenftein renewed his invitation, and preffed them to haften their arrival, but on their journey they learned the bufinefs of Pilfen, which ftopped them. Altringer, under the pretext of ficknefs, remained in the ftrong caftle of Frauenberg; Gallas made his appearance, but it was only the better, as an eye-witnefs, to inform the Emperor of the danger which threatened him; the intelligence which he and Piccolomini gave, changed the fufpicions of the court into the moft alarming certainty; news which arrived from other quarters left no room to doubt,

doubt, and the rapid change of commanders in Silesia and Austria appeared to be the prelude to some great design. So immediate a danger demanded speedy measures; however, it was necessary to proceed with the regular forms. Orders were accordingly issued to the principal generals, on whose fidelity reliance might be placed, to seize Wallenstein and his associates Illo and Terzky, and keep them safe in confinement: but if this could not be done in a quiet manner, the public danger required that they should be taken dead or alive. At the same time General Gallas received a commission, in which the Emperor's orders were made known to the colonels and officers; the whole army was absolved from its obedience to the traitor, and a new generalissimo was appointed in the person of Gallas. In order to bring back the deluded to their duty, and not to plunge the guilty into despair, a general amnesty was granted for all which had been transacted at Pilsen against the majesty of the Emperor.

General Gallas was not pleased with the honour which was done him. He was at Pilsen, under the person whose destiny he was to decide; in the power of an enemy who had

an

an hundred eyes to watch and to difcover his
intentions; if Wallenftein once learnt in whofe
hands he was, nothing could fave him from
the effects of the former's rage and defpair. If
it was prudent to conceal the Emperor's orders,
it was much more difficult to execute them;
the fentiments of the generals were uncertain,
and it was at leaft to be fufpected, that they
would be ready, after the ftep they had taken,
to truft to the Emperor's promifes, and at once
to relinquifh the brilliant expectations they
had formed from Wallenftein. It was alfo a
dangerous enterprife to lay hands upon the perfon of a man who was in a manner confidered
facred, who had long exercifed fupreme authority, who was become the object of the deepeft
veneration, and was armed with every attribute
of outward majefty and interior greatnefs;
whofe very afpect infpired terror, and whofe
wink decided life and death. To feize fuch a
man in the midft of his guards, and in a city
entirely devoted to him, as a criminal, and to
convert the object of long veneration at once
into that of compaffion or reproach, was a
commiffion fufficient to deter the boldeft: fo
deep was the fear and the refpect which the
foldiers entertained of him, that even the atrocious

cious crime of high treason could not eradicate these sentiments.

Gallas perceived the impossibility of executing his commission under the eyes of Wallenstein, and was desirous, before he proceeded further, to consult Altringer. As the delay of the latter began **to excite** suspicion, Gallas offered to repair to Frauenberg, and as a relation prevail upon him to return; Wallenstein received this mark of his zeal with such satisfaction, **that** he lent him his own equipage to perform the journey. Gallas rejoiced that his stratagem succeeded, immediately left Pilsen, while Piccolomini remained to watch Wallenstein's motions: but he did not fail, wherever he went, to use the Emperor's commission, and the declaration of the troops was more favourable than he expected. Instead of bringing back his friend, he sent him to Vienna to inform the Emperor of his danger, and went himself to Upper Austria, which was threatened **by** the approach of the Duke of Weimar: in Bohemia Imperial garrisons were thrown into the towns of Budweiss and Tabor, and every measure **was** taken effectually to oppose the designs of the traitor.

As

As Gallas intended no more to return, Piccolomini determined to put Wallenstein's credulity once more to the test; he demanded permission to bring back Gallas, and Wallenstein suffered himself a second time to be deceived. This inconceivable blindness is only to be considered as the offspring of pride, which never retracted the opinion it had formed of a person, and could not be brought to acknowledge its error; he even sent Piccolomini in his own coach to Lintz, where the latter immediately followed the example of Gallas, and went one step further. He had promised Wallenstein to return: this, however, he did at the head of an army, with the intention of falling upon the former at Pilsen: another army, under General Snys, hastened to Prague, to secure that capital, and defend it against an attack of the rebels. At the same time Gallas announced himself as commander in chief to the different Imperial armies in Germany, and issued orders accordingly; bills were posted up in all the Imperial camps, raising the hue and cry against Wallenstein and four of his associates, and releasing the troops from their obedience to him.

The

The example given at Lintz was univerfally followed; the traitor was generally detefted, and forfaken by all the armies. At length, as Piccolomini no longer returned, Wallenftein was undeceived, and he recovered in confternation from his dream; yet he ftill continued to believe in the predictions of aftrology and the fidelity of the army. Immediately after Piccolomini's defection, he gave out an order that no command fhould in future be obeyed which did not proceed from either himfelf, Terzky, or Illo; he haftily prepared to advance towards Prague, where he intended to throw off the mafk, and openly declare againft the Emperor. All the troops were to have affembled before Prague, and inftantly to have proceeded from thence into Auftria; the Duke of Weimar, who was led into the confpiracy, was to have fupported Wallenftein's operations with Swedifh troops, and make a diverfion upon the Danube; Terzky already haftened towards Prague, and it was the want of horfes alone which prevented Wallenftein from following him with the faithful regiments. But while with the moft exceffive hope he awaited for intelligence from Prague, he received information of the lofs of that city, the defection of his generals, the defertion of his troops, the

difcovery

discovery of his conspiracy, and the sudden march of Piccolomini, who vowed him destruction; all his designs were defeated on a sudden, and his prospects annihilated; he now saw himself alone, forsaken by all to whom he had been a benefactor, and betrayed by those on whom he placed dependance. But it is in such situations that great characters are proved. Though deceived in all his expectations, he did not abandon one of his designs; he despaired of nothing so long as he himself lived. The period was at length arrived when he wanted that support for which he had so often applied to the Swedes and Saxons, and when every doubt disappeared as to the sincerity of his intentions. After Oxenstern and Arnheim perceived the truth of his promised intentions and his necessity, they hesitated no longer to embrace the favourable opportunity, and offer him their protection. It was resolved to detach the Duke of Saxe Lauenburg with 4000 men from the Saxons, and the Palatine of Birkenfeld with 6000 Swedes, all chosen troops, to his assistance. Wallenstein left Pilsen with Terzky's regiment, and the few who either were or pretended to remain faithful to him, and hastened to Egra in order to be near the Upper Palatinate, and facilitate his junction

with

with the Duke of Weimar. He was not yet acquainted with the decree which proclaimed him an enemy and a traitor; he first received this thunder-stroke at Egra. He still confided in an army which General Schafgotsch prepared for him in Silesia, and flattered himself with hopes that many of those who had forsaken him would return upon the first dawnings of success; even during his flight to Egra, so little humility was he taught by sad experience, that he was still occupied by the colossal scheme of deposing the Emperor. It was in these circumstances that one of his attendants asked him leave to offer advice: "Under the Emperor," said he, "your Grace is a great and much "esteemed lord; joined with the enemy, you "are at best but a precarious king. It is not "the part of prudence to exchange certainty "for uncertainty. The enemy will make them- "selves masters of your person when the oppor- "tunity offers. You will be ever an object of "their suspicions, lest you should act one day "as the Emperor now does: on that account "return to your allegiance while it is yet "time."—"And what is the remedy?" said Wallenstein. "You have," replied the other, "40,000 men in arms" (meaning ducats,

stamped

stamped with the figure of a man in armour):
„ take them with you, and go straight to the
" Imperial court; there declare that the steps
" which you have hitherto taken were merely
" to put the fidelity of the Emperor's subjects
" to the test, and distinguish the loyal from
" the suspicious; and since most showed a
" disposition to rebel, say you are come to
" warn his Imperial Majesty against these dan-
" gerous men. By this you will make your
" enemies appear as traitors, your ducats will
" make you a welcome guest at the Imperial
" court, and you will be reinstated in your
" former dignity."—" The advice is good,"
answered Wallenstein after a pause, " but the
" d—l trust to it."

While Wallenstein was actively negotiating with the enemy at Egra, consulting the stars and indulging new hopes, the poniard was drawn almost before his eyes which put a period to his existence. The Imperial proclamation which set a price upon his head, had not failed in its effect, and fate ordained that one act of ingratitude should be punished by another. Among his officers, Wallenstein had in particular distinguished one Leslie, an Irishman, and made his fortune.

tune. This man, whether from a sense of duty or a meaner impulse, felt himself called on to execute the sentence against Wallenstein; and to merit the bloody reward. He was no sooner arrived at Egra, in Wallenstein's suite, than he disclosed to the governor, Colonel Butler, and to Lieutenant-colonel Gordon, two Protestant Scotchmen*, all the dangerous designs which that infatuated man had the imprudence to impart on his way thither. Leslie here found two men fit for his design; they had the alternative of duty or treason, of adhering to their lawful sovereign, or to a fugitive abandoned rebel; and although the latter was an universal benefactor, the choice could not remain doubtful for an instant; they were solemnly bound in their allegiance to the Emperor, and this required them to take immediate measures against the common enemy. But not to offend justice, it was determined to deliver up her victim alive, and the conspirators parted with the bold project of taking the General prisoner. This dark plot was covered

---

* Here the author is mistaken. Butler was an Irishman and a Papist; he died a general in the Emperor's service. Though a murderer, he was a man of great piety, and founded at Prague a convent of Irish Franciscans, which still exists. *Transf.*

with

with the deepest secrecy; and Wallenstein, instead of entertaining the least surmise of his impending destruction, rather flattered himself that he possessed in the garrison of Egra his bravest and most faithful adherents.

At this time were brought him the Imperial proclamations which contained his sentence, and were made public in all the camps. He now perceived the greatness of the danger with which he was surrounded, the impossibility of a retreat, his dreadful situation, and the absolute necessity of delivering himself up to the enemy. He imparted to Leslie the chagrin of his afflicted soul, and the violent effect of the moment drew from him the last remaining secret. He disclosed to this officer his intention of delivering up Egra and Elnbogen, the passes of the kingdom, to the Palatine of Birkenfeld; and at the same time informed him of the Duke of Weimar's approach, of which he had advice the same night by a messenger. This discovery, which Leslie immediately communicated to the other conspirators, altered their plan; the pressing danger no longer permitted dilatory measures; Egra might every moment fall into the enemy's hands, and a sudden revolution release their prisoner. To prevent

prevent this, they determined to assassinate him and his associates the next night.

In order to execute this design with the less noise, it was determined that the act should be perpetrated at an entertainment which Colonel Butler gave at the castle of Egra. All the guests made their appearance except Wallenstein, who, being too much agitated to enjoy company, sent an apology; with regard to him, therefore, the plan must be changed; but it was resolved to execute the design upon the others. Colonels Illo, Terzky, and William Kinsky, came in a careless confidence, and with them Captain Neuman, an officer of talents, whose advice Terzky demanded in every intricate affair. Previous to their arrival the most confidential soldiers of the garrison were entrusted with the plot and introduced into the castle; all avenues from it were guarded, and six of Butler's dragoons concealed in an apartment near the dining-room, who, on a concerted signal, were to rush out and kill the traitors. Without imagining the danger which hung over them, the unsuspecting guests abandoned themselves to the pleasures of the table, and Wallenstein's health was drank in full bumpers, not as an Imperial general,

general, but a fovereign prince. Wine rendered them more communicative, and Illo boafted with great exultation, that in three days an army would arrive, fuch as Wallenftein had never before commanded. " Yes," added Neuman, " and then he hopes to wafh his hands " in Auftrian blood." At thefe words the deffert was taken away, and Leflie gave the concerted fignal to raife the drawbridges, while he took the keys of the doors; the dining-room was inftantly filled with armed men, who amid the cry of *" Long live Ferdinand!"* placed themfelves behind the chairs of the marked victims. The four immediately fprung from the table with confternation; Kinfky and Terzky were inftantly killed before they could refift, Neuman found an opportunity during the confufion to efcape into the yard, where he was recognifed, and inftantly cut down by the guards; Illo alone had prefence of mind to defend himfelf. He placed his back to a window, from whence he uttered the bittereft reproaches againft Gordon for his treachery, and challenged him to fight him like a gentleman: after a gallant refiftance, during which he killed two of his enemies, he fell to the ground overpowered by numbers, and pierced with ten wounds. Immediately after the action was

commit-

committed, Leslie hastened into the town to anticipate the report; when he was seen by the centinels at the castle-gates running out of breath, they fired their muskets at him, thinking he belonged to the rebels, but without effect: these shots, however, assembled the town-guard, and it required all Leslie's presence of mind to disarm them. He now hastily detailed to them the circumstances of Wallenstein's conspiracy, and the measures which were already taken to oppose it, the fate of the four rebels, together with that which awaited the principal. Finding the troops well disposed to second his design, he exacted from them a new oath of allegiance to the Emperor, to live or die in his cause. A hundred of Butler's dragoons were now detached through the streets, in order to terrify the dependants of the traitor and to prevent tumult: all the gates of Egra were immediately occupied; and every avenue to Wallenstein's residence, which was near the market-place, was guarded by numerous and faithful detachments, which prevented either his escaping or receiving assistance.

Previous, however, to the last step, a long conference was held, in which it was debated whether they should kill him, or content themselves

selves with making him a prisoner. Already covered with the blood of his associates, these furious men hesitated to take away the life of such an illustrious personage; they had seen him their leader in battle, and in his fortunate days surrounded by his victorious army; and the awe to which they had so long been accustomed again seized them. But this emotion was soon suppressed by the impending danger. They remembered the threats which Illo and Neuman threw out at table; the appearance of a formidable Swedish and Saxon army was hourly expected before Egra; and safety was only to be sought in the death of the traitor: they remained stedfast, therefore, to their first resolution; and Captain Devereux, an Irishman, received the bloody orders.

While the three above mentioned decided his fate in the castle of Egra, Wallenstein was occupied in consulting the stars with Seni. *"The danger is not yet over,"* said the astrologer with a prophetic spirit; *"It is,"* answered Wallenstein, who would even contradict the decrees of Heaven; "*but it stands written in* "*the stars that thou shalt soon be thrown into* "*prison!*"

The aftrologer had taken his leave, and Wallenftein was in bed when Devereux with fix halberdiers came to his houfe, and was immediately admitted by the guard, who were accuftomed to fee him go to the general at all hours. A page who met him on the ftairs, and wifhed to raife the alarm, was run through the body with a pike; in the antechamber the affaffins met a fervant who had juft come out of his mafter's apartment, and taken with him the key; by putting his finger to his mouth, the affrighted flave admonifhed them to make no noife, as the general was afleep. "*Friend,*" faid Devereux, "*it is time to awake him;*" with thefe words he ran againft the door, and burft it open.

Wallenftein was aroufed from his firft fleep by the noife of a mufket which went off, and fprung to the window to call the guard; he at the fame time heard the lamentations of the Counteffes Terzky and Kinfky, who had juft learned the violent death of their hufbands. Before he had time for reflection, Devereux with his affaffins was in the apartment; he was in his fhirt, and leaning on a table near the window. "Art thou the villain," cried Devereux, "who intends to deliver up the Empe-
"ror's

"ror's troops to the enemy, and to dethrone "his Majesty? Now thou muſt die." He pauſed a few moments, as if expecting an anſwer; but rage and aſtoniſhment ſilenced Wallenſtein: with arms extended he received in his breaſt the aſſaſſins' halberts, and fell weltering in his blood without **a groan.**

The next day an expreſs arrived from the Duke of Lauenburg, announcing his approach: the meſſenger was ſecured, and a lackey was ſent in Wallenſtein's livery to decoy the Duke into Egra: the ſtratagem ſucceeded, and Francis Albert delivered himſelf up to the enemy. The Duke of Weimar, who was on his march to Egra, was near ſharing the ſame fate; he very fortunately learned Wallenſtein's death in ſufficient time to ſave himſelf by a retreat.

Ferdinand ſhed a tear **over** the fate of his general, and ordered 3000 maſſes to **be ſaid** for his ſoul in Vienna; but did not at the ſame time forget to decorate his aſſaſſins with gold chains, chamberlains' keys, dignities and eſtates.

Thus did Wallenſtein, at the age of fifty years, terminate his active and extraordinary life.

life. Led away by ambition and the love of fame, he was still, with all his failings, an admirable and inimitable character, had he contained himself within bounds. The virtues of the ruler and the hero, prudence, justice, firmness, and courage, are the striking features of his character; but he wanted the softer virtues of humanity, which adorn the hero, and procure the ruler the esteem of mankind. Terror was the talisman with which he worked: excessive in his punishments as well as in his rewards, he knew how to keep the zeal of his followers continually expanded, and no general of ancient or modern times could boast of being obeyed with equal alacrity: obedience was of more real service to him than the soldier's courage, because he acted through its means. He kept his troops in practice by capricious orders, and rewarded a readiness to obey him, even in small matters, with profusion; he at one time issued an order that none but red sashes should be worn in the army. A captain of horse no sooner heard the order than he trampled his gold embroidered sash under foot; Wallenstein, on being informed of this circumstance, promoted him to the rank of colonel upon the spot. With all this appearance of caprice, he did not lose sight of the main object. The robberies of the troops in their friends' country had occasioned

sioned the severest orders against stragglers; and those who were detected in a theft were threatened to be punished with the halter. It happened that Wallenstein himself met a soldier, whom he commanded, without trial, to be taken up as a transgressor, and with his usual stern order of "*Hang the fellow*," condemned him to the gallows; the soldier pleaded innocence, but the decisive sentence was pronounced. "Hang, then, innocent," cried Wallenstein; "the guilty will tremble "with more certainty." Preparations were already making to execute the sentence, when the soldier, who gave himself up for lost, formed the desperate resolution of not dying without revenge. He furiously fell upon his judge, but was soon disarmed by numbers before he could execute his design. "Now let "him go," cried Wallenstein; "he will ex- "cite sufficient terror."

His munificence was supported by an immense income, which was valued at three millions * annually, without reckoning the immoderate sums which he raised by contributions. His freedom of thinking and clearness of un-

* Florins, no doubt. *Transf.*

derstanding

derstanding placed him above the religious prejudices of his age, and the Jesuits could never forgive him for having seen through their system, and beheld nothing in the Pope but a Roman bishop.

But as, since Samuel the prophet's days, no one came to a fortunate end who quarrelled with the church, Wallenstein also augmented its victims. Through monkish intrigues he lost at Ratisbon the command of the army, and at Egra his life; by the same acts he perhaps lost what is more, his honest reputation and his fame with posterity. For it must be candidly acknowledged that we have the history of this extraordinary man delivered to us by no means through impartial hands; and that Wallenstein's treason, and his designs upon the crown of Bohemia, rest less upon any positive proof than upon appearances of probability. We have not yet discovered the documents which might display the secret springs of his conduct with historic truth; and among all the actions ascribed to him openly, there is not one which could not proceed from an innocent source. Many of his most obnoxious measures showed an inclination for peace; others were to be excused by his just suspicion of the Emperor,

peror, and the blamelefs defire of maintaining his authority. It is true that his conduct towards the Elector of Bavaria bears the appearance of an ignoble revenge and implacable fpirit; but none of his actions clearly convince us of his treafon. When neceffity and defpair at length drove him to merit the fentence which had fallen upon him when innocent, fuch a fentence cannot altogether be juftified; it was his ruin that caufed his rebellion, not rebellion his ruin. Unfortunate while living, he made a victorious party his enemy; equally fo at his death, fince the fame party furvived him, and wrote his hiftory.

Guftavus Adolphus and Wallenftein, the two great heroes of the warlike drama, have now difappeared from the fcene, and with them we lofe that unity of action which has hitherto diftinguifhed the view of affairs. Henceforward a variety of characters attract notice, and the remainder of the war, though more fertile in battles and negotiations, in ftatefmen and heroes, is lefs amufing and interefting for my readers.

CONTINUATION.

Wallenstein's death rendered a new generalissimo necessary, and the Emperor at length was prevailed upon by the Court of Spain to promote his son, Ferdinand King of Hungary, to that rank. Under him General Gallas directed, however, the entire command. A considerable force soon assembled under Ferdinand's colours, the Duke of Lorrain led reinforcements in person, and the Cardinal Infant joined with 10,000 men from Italy. In order to drive the enemy from the Danube, the new general undertook, what his predecessor failed in, the siege of Ratisbon. It was in vain that the Duke of Weimar penetrated into the interior of Bavaria, with a view to draw the enemy's attention from that city: Ferdinand persevered in the siege, and Ratisbon, after the most vigorous resistance, surrendered. Donauwerth soon after shared the same fate, and Nordlingen in Suabia was at length besieged. The loss of so many Imperial cities, whose alliance had hitherto been so advantageous to the Swedes, could not be regarded with indifference. It would have exposed them to great disgrace

if

if they abandoned their allies to an implacable enemy. From these considerations the Swedish army, under General Horn and the Duke of Weimar, advanced towards Nordlingen, determined to relieve it, even at the expense of a battle.

This undertaking was highly imprudent, as the enemy was manifestly superior in number to the Swedes, and foresight required the latter to avoid a battle, the more as the force of the Imperialists was soon to divide itself, and the Italian troops were destined for the Netherlands. It was possible to occupy a position which might cover Nordlingen, and cut off the enemy's supplies. All these considerations were represented by Gustavus Horn in the Swedish council of war; but his remonstrances were disregarded by men who, intoxicated by a long series of successes, saw nothing in the suggestions of prudence but the effects of timidity. Overcome by the superior influence of the Duke of Weimar, Horn was obliged, against his consent, to risk a contest of which he already foresaw the unfavourable issue.

The fate of the battle depended upon the possession of a height which commanded the

Imperial

Imperial camp. An attempt to occupy it during the night failed, as the tedious transport of the artillery through woods and hollow ways necessarily delayed the troops on their march. When the Swedes arrived there about midnight they found the hill already occupied and strongly intrenched by the Imperialists. Daybreak was awaited in order to storm it. The impetuous valour of the Swedes fortunately surmounted the intrenchments, formed in a crescent; but having entered on both sides, they met and fell into confusion. At this unfortunate instant a barrel of powder blew up, and caused great destruction among the Swedes. The Imperial cavalry charged them, and the confusion became general; no efforts of their general could prevail upon the fugitives to renew the attack.

He now endeavoured to maintain this important post, by leading up fresh troops; but some Spanish regiments had already occupied it, and every attempt to gain it was repulsed by the heroic intrepidity of these troops *. One of the

---

* It is remarkable, that the Spanish infantry, now so contemptible, were then the first in the world. All their glory, however, terminated a few years after this by the ever-memorable

the Duke of Weimar's regiments seven times renewed the attack, and was as often repulsed. The disadvantage of not occupying this post was soon perceived. The fire of the enemy's cannon committed such slaughter in the next wing of the Swedes, that Horn, who commanded, was compelled to retire. Instead of covering the retreat of his colleague, the Duke of Weimar was closely pursued into the plain, where his routed cavalry spread confusion among Horn's troops, and rendered the defeat general. Almost the entire infantry was either cut to pieces or taken prisoners; above 12,000 men remained dead upon the field of battle; eighty cannon, 4000 waggons, and 300 standards and colours, fell into the hands of the Imperialists. Horn and three other generals were taken prisoners. The Duke of Weimar with difficulty saved some feeble remains of the army, who joined him in Frankfort.

The defeat at Nordlingen cost Oxenstern

morable victory which the Duke of Enguien gained over them, at the age of twenty-two, at Rocroi—a blow from which Spain never afterwards recovered. The Dutch subsequently became famous for a discipline which has since been carried to the last perfection by the German infantry. *Transf.*

the second sleepless night in Germany *. The consequences of this disaster were terrible. The Swedes at once lost by it their superiority in the field, and with it the allies to whom they had hitherto been indebted for their successes. A dangerous division threatened the Protestant confederacy with ruin. Consternation seized the whole party, and the Catholics arose in exulting triumph from their fall. Suabia and the neighbouring circles first felt the consequences of the defeat at Nordlingen, and Wirtemberg in particular was overrun by the victorious army. All the members of the confederacy of Hailbron trembled before the Emperor's indignation, numbers fled to Strasburg, and the helpless free cities awaited their fate with fear and astonishment. Somewhat greater moderation on the part of the conquerors would have reduced the weaker states under the Emperor's subjection. But the severity which was practised even against those who voluntarily surrendered, made the remainder desperate, and encouraged them to the most vigorous resistance.

Recourse was had upon this occasion to Oxenstern for his counsel and assistance; for

* See the Appendix.

both

both of which he called upon the states of Germany. Armies were wanting; money was also required to raise new troops, and pay off the old arrears. Oxenstern applied to the Elector of Saxony, who shamefully abandoned him, and concluded a treaty of peace with the Emperor at Pirna. He also made application for assistance to the states of Lower Saxony; but the latter, long tired of the Swedish demands, only provided for their own safety; and George Duke of Lunenburg, instead of hastening to the assistance of Upper Germany, laid siege to Minden, with the intention of keeping it for himself. Abandoned by his German allies, the Chancellor applied to foreign powers for assistance. England, Holland, and Venice, were solicited for money and troops; and, driven to the last necessity, he at length resolved to throw himself under the protection of France; a measure which he embraced with reluctance.

The period was at length arrived which Richelieu long waited for with impatience. It was only the impossibility of saving themselves by any other means, that could lead the Protestant states of Germany to second the claims of France on Alsace. Such a necessity now presented

presented itself: the assistance of that power was absolutely requisite, and France was amply paid for the active part which it from this period took in the war. It opened its political career with splendour and reputation; Oxenstiern, whom it cost but little to bestow the rights and possessions of the Empire, had already ceded Philipsburg and other places which were required by Richelieu. The Upper German Protestants now sent a special embassy to him to take Alsace, the fortress of Brisach, which was still in the enemy's possession, and all the fortified places of the Upper Rhine which commanded the entrance into Germany, under his protection. France was already in possession of the bishoprics of Metz, Toul, and Verdun, which it defended for centuries against their lawful proprietors. Treves was in its power; Lorrain was in a manner conquered, as it might every moment be overrun by an army, and could not, by its native strength, withstand the force of its powerful neighbour. France now enjoyed the prospect of adding Alsace to its numerous possessions, and as it, at the same time, entered into a treaty with the Dutch for the division of the Spanish Netherlands, it could expect to make the Rhine its natural barrier against the Emperor. So shamefully

fully were the possessions of Germany sold by its states to that faithless avaricious power, which, under the mask of disinterested friendship, only laboured for aggrandizement; and while it claimed the respectable title of a protectress, was only employed in promoting its own views, amid the general confusion.

In return for these important cessions, France engaged to make a diversion in favour of the Swedes, by commencing hostilities against the Spaniards; and, should it come to an open breach with the Emperor, to maintain an army of 12,000 men upon the opposite side of the Rhine, which was to act, in conjunction with the Swedes, against Austria. The desired pretext for a war was given by the Spaniards themselves. They made an inroad from the Netherlands into Treves, cut in pieces the French garrison which lay in that city, and took prisoner, in violation of the laws of nations, the Elector, who had put himself under the protection of France, and brought him to Flanders. When the Cardinal Infant, as viceroy of the Spanish Netherlands, refused satisfaction for those injuries, and delayed to restore the prince, whom he had taken, to his liberty, Richelieu, after the old custom, formally declared war against him by a herald.

a herald whom he sent to Brussels, and immediately commenced it by three different armies in Italy and Flanders. The French minister was not so ready to begin against the Emperor a war which promised few advantages, and was accompanied with great difficulties. Nevertheless a fourth army was detached over the Rhine into Germany, under the Cardinal La Valette, to act in conjunction with the Duke of Weimar, without a previous declaration of war against the Emperor.

Ferdinand's reconciliation with the Elector of Saxony was a more severe blow to the Swedes than their defeat at Nordlingen. After a fruitless attempt to prevent it, this negotiation was concluded during the winter 1634, at Pirna, and ended the following May in a formal peace. The Elector of Saxony could never conceal his aversion to that foreign power which gave laws to Germany, and his hatred was increased by every new demand of Oxenstern. This aversion to Sweden was increased by the efforts of the Court of Spain, who laboured to effect a treaty between Saxony and the Emperor. Wearied by the calamities of a long and destructive war, which made Saxony above all other countries its theatre, excited by

the

the miseries which both friends and enemies heaped upon his subjects, and seduced by the deceitful offers of Austria, the Elector at last abandoned the common cause; and less occupied by Germany's liberty than his own safety, only consulted the latter.

In fact, misery had risen in Germany to such a pitch, that all voices exclaimed for a peace, even the most disadvantageous. In plains which had formerly possessed plenty and happiness, and over which thousands of people were spread, nothing but devastation was now to be seen; the fields, abandoned by the industrious husbandman, lay waste and uncultivated, and where a young crop or a smiling harvest appeared, a march of soldiers destroyed the fruits of a twelvemonth's labour. Burned castles and villages in ashes lay upon all sides the melancholy objects of contemplation, while their plundered inhabitants repaired to join an army of incendiaries, and retaliate upon their fellow-citizens that fate to which they themselves had been the first victims. In order to avoid oppression, recourse was had to violence. The towns groaned under the licentiousness of undisciplined garrisons, who squandered the property of the inhabitants, and exercised the utmost disorders. While the march of an army laid waste an entire country, or plundered it by winter-quarters or contributions, the industry of a whole year was effaced by the ravages of a month. The fate of such as had a garrison within their walls, or in their neighbourhood, was the most unhappy, because the victors trod in the footsteps of the vanquished, and no greater indulgence was to be expected from friends than from enemies. All these different calamities brought want and hunger to their utmost pitch, and the miseries of the latter years were increased by a sterility*. The crowding of people in camps and quarters, want upon one side, and excess on the other, occasioned contagious distempers, which were more fatal than the sword. All the bonds of social life were dissolved in this universal confusion; the respect for order, the fear of the laws, the purity of morals and of religion, were

* In the year 1634, when the negotiations were opened at Pirna, provisions became so dear, that an egg was sold for six creitzers (three halfpence English), a much greater sum in those days than at present, in Germany; a pound of meat, ten and twenty creitzers; a bushel of oats, sixteen rix-dollars; and one of barley, thirty. A fowl cost a florin, and a Nuremberg cask of wine twenty rix-dollars (3*l.* 5*s.*). *Author.*

lost

lost under the weight of an iron sceptre. Anarchy and impunity disdained every law, and men became ferocious according as their country was wasted. No situation was longer respected, no property was secured from plunder. The soldier, in a word, reigned, and that most brutal of despots often made his superiors experience his own power. The general was the most important personage, and the legal proprietor of a country was often obliged to fly to his castles for safety. The whole of Germany swarmed with these petty tyrants, and the country suffered equally from friends and enemies. All those wounds were the more severe, on reflecting that it was foreign powers who sacrificed the country to their ambition, and encouraged the miseries of the war only to pursue their own advantages. Germany bled in order to promote the interests of Sweden; and Richelieu's alliance was indispensable.

But it was not interested voices alone who were against a peace: while both Swedes and Germans declared for a continuance of the war, they were seconded by a sound policy. An advantageous peace with the Emperor was not to be expected after the defeat at Nordlingen; and it was too great a sacrifice to have gained nothing, or rather lost every thing, after a seventeen years contest. So much blood was unnecessarily shed without attaining its object. It was more reasonable to prosecute the war, and support the burden for some period longer, than to surrender the advantages which had been obtained. A fortunate peace was to be expected when the Swedes and German Protestants unanimously pursued their interests as well in the cabinet as in the field. It was their division which alone rendered the enemy formidable: this greatest of all evils was occasioned by the Elector of Saxony, when he concluded a separate peace.

He had already commenced a negotiation with the Emperor previous to the defeat at Nordlingen, an event which accelerated the treaty. All confidence in the Swedes was lost, and it was doubted whether they should ever recover their late blow. No further exploits were expected from the division of their commanders, the insubordination of the armies, and the decay of Sweden. It was upon this account thought the more expedient to profit by the Emperor's magnanimity, who withdrew his pretensions after the victory which he had
obtained

obtained at Nordlingen. Oxenstern, who assembled the states at Frankfort, made demands; the Emperor, on the contrary, yielded; so that men did not long hesitate which party to embrace.

But, to save appearances, an anxiety for the common cause was affected. All the states of Germany, and even the Swedes, were publicly invited to partake in this peace, although it only was concluded between the Emperor and the Elector of Saxony, who assumed the power of giving law to Germany. The grievances of the Protestant states were here debated, their rights and privileges decided before this arbitrary tribunal, and the fate of their religion resolved upon without consulting the members who were so much interested in it. A formal peace was determined upon, and to enforce it by an army of execution as a regular decree of the Empire. Whoever opposed this measure was to be considered as a public enemy. The treaty of Prague was thus, even in form, a work of caprice, neither was it less so in its contents.

The edict of restitution had chiefly caused the breach between the Emperor and the Elector of Saxony, and it was therefore taken first into confideration at their reconciliation; without formally abolifhing it, the treaty of Prague determined that all the chapters which the Proteftants had feized after the negotiation at Paffau, fhould remain during forty years in the fame condition in which they were when the edict of reftitution was iffued. Before this term was elapfed, a committee of both religions was to be appointed, who fhould regularly proceed to decide the common affairs; and if they did not conclude a treaty, both parties were to remain poffeffed of the rights which they maintained previous to the edict. It was thus that this treaty, far from concluding a formal peace, only covered the embers of a war.

The bifhopric of Magdeburg was ceded to Prince Auguftus of Saxony, and Halberftadt to the Archduke Leopold William: four eftates were taken from the territory of Magdeburg and given to Saxony: the Adminiftrator of Magdeburg, Chriftian William of Brandenburg, was indemnified in another manner. The Dukes of Mecklenburg were to recover, by joining in the peace, their territories which they had already been fortunately poffeffed of

by

by means of Guſtavus Adolphus. Donauwerth recovered its liberty. The claims of the Palatine heirs, however important for the Proteſtant cauſe, remained unnoticed from the animoſity which ſubſiſted between a Lutheran and a Calviniſt party. All conqueſts were mutually reſtored, and Sweden and France were forcibly to yield the poſſeſſions which they had appropriated to themſelves. It was determined that the contracting parties ſhould aſſemble an army in order to enforce this treaty.

As the treaty of Prague was deſtined for a general law of the Empire, the points which did not more immediately belong to the latter, were contained in a ſeparate article. In this, Luſatia was ceded to the Elector of Saxony as a fief of Bohemia, and the toleration of religion in that country and Sileſia was particularly provided for.

All the Proteſtant ſtates were invited to partake in the treaty, and were upon that condition granted the amneſty. The princes of Wirtemberg and Baden, whoſe territories were in the enemy's poſſeſſion, and who, though the immediate vaſſals of Auſtria, were directed by Oxenſtern, were alone excluded: this was not done

done that the war might be profecuted againſt them, but rather to fell a peace the dearer. It was intended to keep their dominions as a pledge for reſtoring every thing at the concluſion of a peace to its former footing: an equal juſtice towards all the ſtates had, perhaps, promoted the good underſtanding between all parties, and compelled the Swedes to a difgraceful retreat from Germany. But the ſevere treatment of the Proteſtants upon this occaſion, augmented their ſpirit of oppoſition, and facilitated the deſigns of the Swedes.

The treaty of Prague, as **was** expected, was received throughout Germany with various emotions. The efforts which were made to reconcile the hoſtile parties increaſed the reproaches of both; the Proteſtants complained **againſt** the reſtraints which were impoſed upon them, the Catholics murmured againſt the **indulgence with which their enemies were treated.** It was loudly exclaimed that the intereſts **of the** church were ſacrificed, ſince a forty years poſſeſſion of its chapters was formally granted to the Catholics; according to ſome, treachery was manifeſt towards the Proteſtants, becauſe toleration was not obtained for their brethren in the Auſtrian dominions. But no perſon was

was so much reproached as the Elector of Saxony, who was publicly represented as a deserter, a traitor against liberty and religion, and a partisan of the Emperor.

Ferdinand, **meanwhile,** consoled himself that the treaty which he concluded was embraced by most of the Protestant states; it was agreed to by the Elector of Brandenburg, William Duke of Weimar, the Princes of Anhalt, the Dukes of Mecklenburg, those of Brunswic Lunenburg, the Hanse Towns, and most of the Imperial free cities. William Landgrave of Hesse Cassel long wavered, or affected to do so, in order to gain time to conform to circumstances; he had conquered some fertile countries in Westphalia, from whence he drew his chief means of supporting the war, and which, according to the terms of the peace, he was bound to restore. Bernard Duke of Weimar, whose territories existed only upon paper, was considered not as a hostile power, but merely as a general, and in both capacities it was natural for him to detest the treaty of Prague. All that prince's riches consisted in his valour, and his sword was his only fortune; it was the war alone which rendered him important, and gratified his ambition.

But

But among all who declared against the treaty of Prague, none were so loud in their clamours as the Swedes, who were most interested in it. Invited by the Germans themselves, champions of the Protestant religion, and of the German liberties, which they had purchased at the expense of so much blood and by the life of their sovereign, they now beheld themselves abandoned, deceived in their plans, and ungratefully driven out of the Empire; no indemnification or reward was provided for them by the treaty; they were now poorer than on their arrival, and to be driven from Germany by the very powers which invited them. At length the Elector of Saxony spoke of indemnification, and mentioned the small sum of 2,500,000 florins; but the Swedes had rated their services at a higher price, and scorned to accept of a pecuniary recompence. " The " Electors of Bavaria and Saxony," exclaimed Oxenstern, ". are paid for the services which " they render the Emperor with whole pro- " vinces; and are we Swedes, who have already " sacrificed our king for Germany, to be dis- " missed with the small sum of 2,500,000 " florins?" The disappointed expectation was the more painful, as the Swedes flattered themselves with receiving, as a reward of their services,

vices, the dutchy of Pomerania, whose present possessor was old and wanted heirs. But the inheritance of that dutchy was, by the treaty of Prague, secured to the Elector of Brandenburg; and all parties exclaimed against the Swedes obtaining a footing in Germany.

The Swedes had never experienced such a reverse of fortune as during the present year 1635, immediately after the conclusion of the treaty of Prague. Many of their allies, particularly the free cities, forsook them in order to benefit by the peace; others were compelled to it by the victorious arms of the Emperor; Augsburg, perishing with hunger, submitted under severe conditions; Wirtzburg and Coburg yielded to the Emperor; the confederacy of Hailbron was formally dissolved; almost all the south of Germany, which contained the principal force of the Swedes, submitted to the Austrians. Saxony, in consequence of the treaty of Prague, demanded the evacuation of Thuringia, Halberstadt, and Magdeburg; Philipsburg, the French depôt, was surprised, together with all its military stores, and that great loss diminished the activity of France. To complete the embarrassment of Sweden, the cessation of hostilities with Poland was drawing near

near an end; to support a war at the same time with the German empire and with Poland, was an undertaking much above the power of Sweden, who had to make choice of one or the other. Pride and ambition declared in favour of the German war, which threatened to cost a large sacrifice on the side of Poland: an army was at all events necessary to keep Poland in respect, even at the conclusion of a peace, or a cessation of hostilities.

All these misfortunes presented themselves at once to the genius of Oxenstern, so fertile in expedients, and whose penetrating mind knew how to turn even calamity to his advantage. The defection of so many German states from the Swedish party, had deprived him of allies which had hitherto supported him; but at the same time he was released from all obligations towards them, and the more numerous were his enemies, the more his armies could spread and provide themselves with resources. The palpable ingratitude of the states, and the haughty contempt with which he was treated by the Emperor (who did not condescend to negotiate with *him* about a peace), excited in Oxenstern all the feelings of despair and a just indignation. A war, though ever so disadvantageous,

tageous, could not render the situation of the Swedes worse; and if Germany was to be evacuated, it was more reputable to abandon it sword in hand, and to yield to force rather than to fear.

In the great extremity in which the Swedes found themselves by the desertion of their allies, they applied to France, which met them with the most advantageous offers; the interests of both crowns were united, and France, by permitting the ruin of the Swedes in Germany, acted against itself. The bad situation of the Swedes was, perhaps, the motive which induced the French to a closer alliance, and to take a more active part in the war. Since the treaty with Sweden at Beerwalde, in the year 1632, France had stopped the progress of the Imperial arms, through the means of Gustavus Adolphus, without an open breach, and by the subsidies which she gave to the latter; but rendered uneasy by the sudden and extraordinary success of the Swedes, France altered her first plan for some time, in order to re-establish that balance of power which was injured by the superiority of the former. The French endeavoured to save the Catholic princes of the Empire, by making

making them embrace a neutral system, and on the failure of that design, were ready to take up arms against the northern conqueror. But no sooner had the death of Gustavus Adolphus and the adversity of the Swedes dissipated these apprehensions, than France immediately returned to her former system, and afforded that protection to the unfortunate which she denied them under more favourable circumstances. Richelieu, who was freed by the death of the Swedish king from all the opposition with which his schemes for aggrandizement had hitherto met, embraced the favourable opportunity of the defeat at Nordlingen, to obtain himself the entire direction of the war; the conjuncture favoured his boldest projects, and justified schemes which had hitherto appeared chimerical. He accordingly turned all his attention to the German war, and after securing his private plans by an alliance with the Germans, he appeared as a leader upon the political theatre: while the hostile powers exhausted themselves by mutual efforts, France had spared herself, and during ten years carried on the war with money; but now, when the season for activity arrived, Richelieu seized the sword, and displayed efforts which set all Europe in astonishment. He ordered two fleets to cruife upon the feas, and fent out fix different armies, at the fame time that he had in his pay a crown and feveral German princes. Encouraged by fo powerful a protection, the Swedes and Germans recovered from their confternation, and hoped to obtain by the fword a more favourable peace than that of Prague. Abandoned by their confederates, who treated with the Emperor, the Proteftant ftates formed a clofer union with France, which redoubled its fupport with the increafing neceffity, and took a more active, though ftill a private fhare, in the war in Germany, until it at length threw off the mafk, and openly attacked the Emperor.

In order to leave Sweden at full liberty to act againft Germany, France commenced with terminating the Polifh war. By means of the Count d'Avaux its minifter, its concluded an agreement with both powers, which at length was brought about at Stummerfdorf in Pruffia, not without great loffes on the part of the Swedes, who ceded almoft the whole of Polifh Pruffia, which had been purchafed at fuch expenfe by Guftavus Adolphus, and the treaty was prolonged for twenty-fix years; that of Beerwalde was renewed till a future period after

some

some alterations, which the circumstances rendered necessary, first at Compeigne, and then at Wismar and Hamburg: a rupture was already commenced with France in 1635, and by the vigorous attack of that power, the Emperor was deprived of the firmest support from the Netherlands. By supporting the Landgrave of Hesse Cassel and the Duke of Weimar, the Swedes were enabled to act with greater vigour upon the Elbe and the Danube, and the Emperor was compelled to divide his force by a powerful diversion upon the Rhine.

The war was now prosecuted with increasing vigour; and though, by the treaty of Prague, the Emperor lessened the number of his enemies in Germany, he at the same time augmented the zeal and activity of his exterior foes; he had obtained an unlimited influence throughout all the Empire, and was almost absolute master of every state, with a few exceptions. The first effects of this appeared by his procuring for his son Ferdinand III. the dignity of King of the Romans, in which he prevailed by a plurality of voices, notwithstanding the opposition of the heirs of the Elector of Treves, and of the Elector Palatine; but he had exasperated the Swedes to a desperate resistance, and introduced

duced the French into the midſt of Germany. Both crowns now formed a cloſe alliance againſt the Emperor and his confederates. From this period the Swedes, who no longer fought for Germany, but for their own exiſtence, diſplayed no meaſures of diſcretion, and they acted in a more bold and raſh manner; battles, though leſs deciſive, became more bloody and obſtinate; greater exploits, more intrepidity and military ſkill were exhibited: but thoſe events had leſs influence upon the general ſucceſs of the war.

Saxony had engaged by the treaty of Prague to expel the Swedes from Germany; the Saxons became reconciled to the Auſtrians, and joined them. The archbiſhopric of Magdeburg, which had been promiſed to a prince of Saxony, was ſtill in the poſſeſſion of the Swedes, and every attempt to acquire it by negotiation had failed; hoſtilities commenced by the Elector of Saxony's recalling all his ſubjects from Bannier's army, which had encamped upon the Elbe; the officers, long irritated by the want of their arrears, attended this citation, and evacuated one quarter after another. As the Saxons at the ſame time made a movement towards Mecklenburg, in order to take Doemitz, and cut off the

the Swedes from Pomerania and the Baltic; Bannier suddenly marched towards that quarter, relieved Doemitz, and totally defeated the Saxon General Baudissin with 7000 men, one thousand of whom were killed on the spot, and another made prisoners. Reinforced by the troops and artillery which lay in Polish Prussia, and which might be spared from that country since the treaty at Stummersdorf, that brave and impetuous general, the next year, 1636, made an inroad into Saxony, and marked his progress by the most destructive ravages; the unfortunate inhabitants became exposed to the whole force of his indignation; he was exasperated by the former haughtiness of the Saxons while friends, and now still more as enemies. Against the Saxons, the Swedes displayed much greater animosity than against the Austrians and Bavarians, because they opposed the latter only from a sense of duty, while towards the former they showed that the rage of divided friends is the most implacable *. The powerful diversion which the Duke of Weimar and the Landgrave of Hesse Cassel made against the Empe-

---

* An observation confirmed by the experience of ages. The late rebellion in Ireland affords a strong example, where near relations fought on opposite sides, and neither gave nor took quarter. *Transl.*

ror, prevented the latter from affording the neceſſary aſſiſtance to Saxony, and expoſed that electorate to the ravages of Horn's army. At length the Elector having formed a junction with the Imperial General Hatzfeld, advanced againſt Magdeburg, which Horn immediately haſtened to relieve; the united Saxon and Auſtrian armies were now ſpread over the march of Brandenburg, took ſeveral places from the Swedes, and nearly drove them to the Baltic. But contrary to every expectation, Bannier, though given up for loſt, attacked the allied armies on the 24th of September 1636, at Witſtock, where a bloody battle took place. The attack was furious, and the whole force of the enemy was directed againſt the right wing of the Swedes, led on by Bannier in perſon: a deſperate conflict enſued, and there was ſcarce a Swediſh ſquadron which did not return ten times to the charge, and was as often repulſed. When Bannier was at length obliged to yield to the ſuperior numbers of the enemy, his left wing maintained the combat until night, and the ſecond line of the Swedes, which had not come into action, was prepared to renew it the next morning. But the Saxon did not await another attack; his troops were exhauſted by the preceding day's exertions; and as the drivers fled with their horses, his artillery was unserviceable; he accordingly retired the same night with Hatzfeld, and abandoned the field of battle to the Swedes. Above 5000 of the allies were killed upon the spot, without reckoning those who were slaughtered by the Swedish pursuers and the exasperated peasantry; 100 standards and colours, twenty-three cannon, together with the Elector's silver plate, were taken, and 2000 prisoners. This brilliant victory, achieved over a far more numerous and advantageously posted enemy, restored the Swedes at once to their ancient reputation; their enemies trembled, and their allies were inspired with new hopes. Bannier immediately profited by his successes to cross the Elbe, and drove the Austrians before him through Thuringia and Cassel to Westphalia; he then returned, and took up his quarters in Saxony.

But without the assistance which he received from the diversion which the Duke of Weimar and the French made on the Rhine, he could never profit by this splendid victory. The former had, after the defeat at Nordlingen, assembled the remains of the beaten army in Wetterau; but forsaken by his confederates at Hailbron, who were dissolved by the peace

of

of Prague, he could no longer support the army, nor perform great exploits; the defeat at Nordlingen had destroyed all his hopes to obtain the dutchy of Franconia, and the weakness of the Swedes deprived him of the hope of advancing his fortune through their means. Wearied by the constraint which the pretensions of the Swedish Chancellor imposed upon him, he applied to France, who supplied him with money, the article he most wanted. Richelieu desired nothing so much as to remove from the Swedes the conduct of the war, and to place it in his own hands: to attain this end, no means were so expedient as detaching their best general from them, bringing him into the interest of France, and securing the obedience of his army. A prince, such as the Duke of Weimar, who could not exist without foreign support, was the more easily prevailed on to embrace that measure, as he could not remain any considerable time independent of France. The Duke himself went to France, and in October 1635, concluded with Richelieu a treaty at St. Germain en Laye, not for the Swedish general, but in his own name, by which it was stipulated that he was to receive 1,500,000 livres for himself, and 4,000,000 for the subsistence of an army which was to

act

act under the French King's orders. To infpire him with greater zeal, and facilitate the conqueft of Alface, a fecret promife was given him, that that province fhould be fecured to himfelf, a promife which the Duke knew there was no intention of performing. But confiding in his army and his own good fortune, he oppofed one piece of diffimulation to another; if once able to wreft Alface from the enemy, he would not fcruple to defend it alfo againft his ally. With French gold he now raifed an army which acted apparently under France, but which he commanded in reality without entirely abandoning the Swedifh general: he commenced his operations upon the Rhine, where another French army under Cardinal La Valette, had the preceding year, 1635, begun hoftilities.

It was againft this general that the grand Imperial army, after their great victory at Nordlingen, advanced under Gallas, and fortunately drove the French back to Metz, cleared the Rhine of the enemy, and took Mentz and Frankenthal from the Swedes. But Gallas, fruftrated in his defign of taking up his winter-quarters in France by the vigorous refiftance of the French, was compelled to retire to the exhaufted provinces of Alface and Suabia. At the

the opening of the enſuing campaign he however paſſed the Rhine at Briſach, and prepared to remove the war into the interior of France. He actually fell upon Burgundy, while the Spaniards penetrated from the Netherlands into Picardy, and John de Werth, a formidable general and celebrated partiſan, entered Champagne, and ſpread conſternation as far as the gates of Paris. But all the bravery of the Auſtrians failed before an inconſiderable fortreſs in Franche Comté, and they were a ſecond time compelled to abandon their deſigns.

The Duke of Weimar's active genius had been hitherto reſtrained by his dependance on a French general, who was fitter for the prieſthood than the falchion: and although in conjunction with the latter he took Saverne in Alſace, he was not able, in the years 1636 and 1637, to maintain his poſition upon the Rhine. The ill ſucceſs of the French arms in the Netherlands had checked their operations on the Rhine, in Alſace and Briſgau; but in the year 1638 the war took a brilliant turn in theſe parts. Finding himſelf without further conſtraint, and with the unlimited command of his troops, he left, in the beginning of February, his winter-quarters, which he had taken in the

biſhopric

bishopric of Basle, and, contrary to every expectation, advanced towards the Rhine, where nothing less than an attack was expected. The Forest towns of Laufenburg, Waldshut, and Seckingen, were taken in this expedition; and Reinfeld besieged. The commanding general of the Austrians, the Duke of Savelli, repaired by hasty marches to relieve that important place, actually raised its siege, and drove the Duke of Weimar, not without great loss, from before it. But, contrary to all human expectations, the latter appeared the third day after (on the 21st of February 1638) in order of battle, in front of the Imperialists, and while they were enjoying their victory in full security, totally defeated them: in this battle their four generals, Savelli, Werth, Enkenford, and Sperkreiter, together with 2000 men, were taken prisoners. Two of the generals, Werth and Enkenford, Richelieu had afterwards conveyed to France, in order to flatter the vanity of the French nation by the sight of such distinguished captives, and to conceal, under the mask of victory, the public miseries. With this view the standards and colours taken at Reinfeld were brought in solemn procession to the church of our Lady, thrice exhibited before the altar, and committed to sacred custody.

The

The taking of Reinfeld, Roeteln, and Freyburg, were the immediate confequences of the Duke of Weimar's victory. His army confiderably increafed, and his projects expanded in proportion as fortune favoured him. The fortrefs of Brifach, on the Upper Rhine, commanded that river, and was regarded as the key to Alface. No place in that quarter was of more importance to the Auftrians, nor guarded with fuch care. It was to defend it that the Italian army under the Duke of Feria was principally deftined; its ftrength bade defiance to every attack, and the Imperial generals who commanded in that quarter received exprefs orders to hazard every thing in its defence: but the Duke, relying upon his good fortune, refolved to attack this fortrefs. Its ftrength rendering it impregnable, it could only be ftarved into a furrender; and the negligence of its governor, who had converted his provifion of corn into money, expecting no attack, haftened its conqueft. As under thefe circumftances it could not fuftain a long fiege, it muft either be fpeedily relieved or victualled. The Auftrian general Goetz accordingly advanced at the head of 12,000 men, attended by 3000 provifion-waggons, which he intended to have thrown into the place. But he was attacked
with

with vigour by the Duke at Witteveyer, and loft all his corps except 3000 men, together with his entire tranſport. A ſimilar fate was experienced by the Duke of Lorrain at Oxenfeld, near Thann, who, at the head of between 5 and 6000 men, undertook to relieve the fortreſs. After a third ſimilar attempt of General Goetz had failed, Briſach, reduced to the utmoſt extremity by hunger, ſurrendered, after a four months ſiege, on the 7th of December 1638, to its equally obſtinate and humane conqueror.

The conqueſt of Briſach now opened a boundleſs field for the Duke of Weimar's ambition, and his romantic projects became nearly realized. Far from ſurrendering this conqueſt to France, he received its homage in his own name. Intoxicated by his former ſucceſſes, he now imagined that he could depend upon himſelf, and maintain his conqueſt independent of France. At that period, when every thing depended upon courage, when even perſonal ſtrength was of importance, and armies and generals were of more conſequence than provinces, it was natural for a hero, ſuch as the Duke of Weimar, at the head of an excellent army, who felt themſelves under his orders invincible,

vincible, not to be difcouraged in any project. In order to obtain a fupport againft his numerous enemies, he turned his eyes towards Amelia Landgravene of Heffe, widow of the lately-deceafed Landgrave William, a woman of fenfe equal to her courage, who could beftow valuable conquefts, a formidable army, and an extenfive principality, with her hand. By the union of the conquefts of Heffe Caffel with his own upon the Rhine, and the formation of both armies into one, a confiderable power might be maintained in Germany, and perhaps even a third party which might decide the fate of the war. But a fpeedy death terminated thefe extenfive fchemes.

Brifach is ours, cried Richelieu to the Capucin father Jofeph, whom he fent upon a fecond embaffy into Germany; fo much was he tranfported with this pleafing intelligence. He had already intended to demand Alface, Brifgau, and all the advanced provinces of Auftria, without regarding the promife which he had made to the Duke of Weimar. The earneft defire which the latter unequivocally difplayed of maintaining Brifach for himfelf caufed Richelieu the utmoft embarraffment, and every effort was made to retain the Duke

in

in the interest of France. He was invited to court in order to receive the honours due to his triumph:—but he perceived the artifice, and eluded it. He was even honoured by an invitation to espouse the Cardinal's niece; but the proud German prince scorned to contaminate the Saxon blood by an inferior marriage. He was now regarded as a dangerous enemy, and treated as such; his subsidies were withdrawn; and the governor of Brisach, together with his principal officers, were bribed (at least after the Duke's death) of secure his troops and his conquests. These artifices were no secret to the Duke, and the measures which he embraced in the conquered places betrayed his distrust of France. But this quarrel with the French court had the worst effect upon his future operations. The preparations which he made to defend his conquests against an attack of the French compelled him to divide his force; and the loss of his subsidies delayed his appearance in the field. His intention was to pass the Rhine, to relieve the Swedes, and, on the banks of the Danube, to attack the Emperor and Bavaria. He had already disclosed his projects to Bannier, who was preparing to carry the war into Austria, and promised to relieve him, when his sudden death at Neuburg

burg on the Rhine, in July 1639, terminated, in the thirty-fixth year of his age, the immortal career of a hero.

He died of a diforder refembling the plague, which, within two days, carried off 400 men in the camp. The black fpots which appeared upon his corpfe, his own declaration upon his death-bed, and the advantages which France could derive from his deceafe, excited a fufpicion that he was removed by poifon; but this was effectually contradicted by the fymptoms of his diforder. In him the allies loft their greateft general fince Guftavus Adolphus, France a dangerous competitor for Alface, and the Emperor a moft formidable enemy. Formed in the fchool of Guftavus Adolphus a hero and a general, he fuccefsfully imitated his great mafter, and a longer life alone was wanting to prevent the copy from equalling, if not furpaffing, the original. With all the impetuous courage of a foldier he united the cool and firm penetration of a general, the perfevering valour of a man with the boldnefs of youth, the fire of a warrior with all the graceful dignity of a prince, the prudence of a wife man with the confcientioufnefs of a man of honour. Difcouraged by no misfortune, he recovered from his defeats with rapidity and vigour, undismayed by no obstacles or disappointments. His genius soared, perhaps, to a height which could not be attained by any human efforts; but such men are directed by other motives than those which visibly guide ordinary capacities; and, conscious of his own capacity, he formed plans which would be imprudent in most men. Bernard affords, in modern history, a beautiful image of those ages of chivalry when personal valour prevailed, individual prowess conquered provinces, and the feats of a German knight raised him to the Imperial throne.

The best part of the Duke's possessions was his army, which, together with Alsace, he bequeathed to his brother William. But France and Sweden thought they had well-grounded claims upon this army; the latter, because it was raised in his name, and the former because by its means it was supported. Even the Electoral Prince of the Palatinate sought to employ it in the reconquest of his dominions, and tampered with it, first by his agents and then in person. Attempts were made on the part of Austria to win this army; a circumstance the less surprising when we reflect that the justice of the cause was then less considered than its

recompence,

recompence, and courage, like other commodities, was difpofed of to the higheft bidder. But France, richer and more determined, outbid the competitors: it bought over General Erlach, who commanded at Brifach, and the other chiefs, who delivered up that fortrefs, together with the entire army. The young Count Palatine, Charles Louis, who had already made an unfortunate campaign againft the Emperor, was now deceived in his hopes. In order to be a witnefs of this bad fervice which France rendered him, he imprudently entered that kingdom, and ftill more imprudently concealed his name. The Cardinal, who dreaded the juft caufe of the Palatine, was ready to embrace any meafure to fruftrate his defigns. He accordingly had him feized, in breach of the laws of nations, at Moulin, and did not reftore him to liberty until he was informed of the purchafe of Weimar's troops. France now faw itfelf poffeffed of a confiderable force in Germany; and from this moment commenced an open war with the Emperor.

But it was no longer Ferdinand II. whom the French had to oppofe; that prince had died in February 1637, in the 59th year of his age. The war which his ambition had excited furvived him. During an eighteen years reign he had never laid afide the fword, nor tafted the bleffings of peace. He was a prince endowed with the talents of a good fovereign, which might be turned towards the benefit of his fubjects. Mild and humane by nature, but entertaining a wrong idea of his prerogative, he was the inftrument of other men's paffions: he failed in his good intentions; and the friend of juftice was converted into the oppreffor of mankind, the enemy of peace, and the fcourge of his people. Amiable in private life and refpectable as a fovereign, he was only ill-advifed in his politics; and while he obtained the efteem of the Catholics, he drew down upon him the execration of the Proteftants. Hiftory has reprefented to us more wicked defpots than Ferdinand II. but he alone had the fingular fate of kindling a *thirty years war*; but his ambition muft, in order to excite fuch evil confequences, have unfortunately coincided with the period and the prejudices of the times. At a more peaceful period his ambition could not have fucceeded, and the age might have enjoyed tranquillity; but now a fpark unfortunately fell upon the long-prepared combuftibles, and Europe was fet in a blaze.

His

His son Ferdinand III. who a few months before had been raised to the dignity of King of the Romans, inherited his throne, his principles, and his war. But Ferdinand III. had beheld, at a closer view, the miseries of the people and the devastation of the country, and saw the necessity of a peace. Less governed by the Jesuits and the Spaniards, and more moderate towards other religions, he was more susceptible than his father of hearkening to the voice of reason. He accordingly listened to it, and granted a peace to Europe; but not until after a contest of eleven years with the sword and the pen, when he found resistance vain, and necessity had dictated it to him.

Fortune attended his accession to the throne, and his arms were victorious against the Swedes. The latter had, under Bannier's vigorous orders, taken up their winter-quarters in Saxony, after their victory at Wittstock, and opened the campaign of 1637 by the siege of Leipzig. The brave defence of the garrison, and the approach of the Imperial and Electoral troops, saved that city; and Bannier, in order to avoid being cut off from the Elbe, retired to Torgau. But the superiority of the Imperialists also drove him thence; and surrounded by the enemy, interrupted by rivers, and pressed by hunger, he was compelled to undertake a perilous retreat into Pomerania, the boldness and fortunate issue of which border upon romance. The whole army waded through a shallow part of the Oder at Furstenburg, and the men drew the artillery when the horses became disabled. Bannier had expected to find General Wrangel upon the other side of the Oder, and in conjunction with him to attack the enemy. Wrangel appeared not, but in his stead an Imperial army was posted at Landsberg, to cut off the retreat of the Swedes. Bannier now saw he had got into a dangerous snare, from which he could not extricate himself. At his rear lay an exhausted country, and on his left the Austrians and the Oder, which was guarded by the Imperial general Bucheim, and did not afford a passage. He had before his front Landsberg, Custrin, the Warta, and an enemy's army; Poland, which, notwithstanding the truce, he could not trust, was on his right. It is not surprising, if in such a situation he gave himself up for lost, and that the Imperialists already triumphed in his inevitable destruction. Bannier, with just indignation, accused the French as the authors of his misfortune. They had neglected to make, according to to their promise, a diversion upon the Rhine; and their inactivity enabled the Emperor to employ his whole force against the Swedes. "If we are one day," exclaimed the incensed general to the French commissioner, who followed the Swedish camp, "to join the Ger-"mans in a war with France, we shall cross "the Rhine with less ceremony." But reproaches were now expended in vain, when circumstances required an immediate resolution. In order, by stratagem, to draw the enemy from the Oder, he pretended to direct his march towards Poland, and actually sent by that route a great part of the baggage, together with his wife, and the rest of the officers ladies. The Imperialists immediately broke off towards the frontiers of Poland, to intercept his retreat; and Bucheim forsook his position, by which the Oder was cleared. Bannier on a sudden, taking advantage of the night, returned to that river, and crossed it a mile above Custrin, with baggage and artillery, without either boats or bridges, in the same manner as he had done at Furstenburg. He arrived without loss in Pomerania, to defend which Wrangel and he were now occupied.

But

But the Imperialists under the command of Gallas entered that dutchy at Ribses, and overran it with their superior strength; Usedom and Wolgast were taken by storm, Demmin by capitulation; and the Swedes were driven to Lower Pomerania. It was now more than ever of consequence to maintain a footing in this dutchy, as at that period its Duke Bogislas XVII. had died, and the Swedes resolved to enforce their claims to Pomerania. In order to prevent the Elector of Brandenburg from establishing his right to the succession of that dutchy, which he was also promised by the treaty of Prague, Sweden exerted all her strength, and vigorously supported her generals both with men and money. In other parts of the Empire, the affairs of the Swedes began to assume a more favourable aspect, and gradually recovered from the humiliating situation in which the inactivity of France and the desertion of their allies had placed them; they had lost every post in Upper Saxony after their retreat to Pomerania; the Dukes of Mecklenburg, terrified by the Imperial arms, began to incline to the Emperor's party, and even George Duke of Lunenburg openly declared for him. Ehrenbreitstein was starved to a surrender by the Bavarian general Werth, and the Austrians

possessed

possessed themselves of all the works which were thrown up on the Rhine; France had lost in its contest with Spain, and the issue by no means answered the pompous expectations which were formed on commencing the war with the latter power; every place was lost which the Swedes possessed in the interior of Germany, and they still maintained only the principal towns in Pomerania. One single campaign recovered them from all these calamities, and the powerful diversion which the Duke of Weimar made on the Rhine at once gave a new turn to the war.

The quarrels between France and Sweden were at length laid aside, and the old treaty between these crowns was renewed at Hamburg with new advantages for the Swedes. In Hesse Cassel the politic Landgravine Amelia, having obtained the consent of the states, assumed the reins of government after the demise of her husband, and resolutely maintained her rights against the Emperor and the line of Darmstadt. The Swedish Protestant party, zealously devoted to their religion, only awaited a favourable moment to declare themselves; they in the mean time succeeded by artfully prolonging a negotiation with the Emperor,

peror, to gain time until their private treaty was concluded with France, and the Duke of Weimar's victories had effected a fortunate change in the affairs of the Protestants; they then threw off the mask, and publicly renewed their old friendship with Sweden. The Duke of Weimar's success even encouraged the Palatine Prince to seek his fortune against the common enemy; with English gold he raised troops in Holland, formed a magazine at Meppen, and united in Westphalia with the Swedish troops. His magazine was in fact lost; his army was defeated by General Hatzfeld at Flotha; but his expedition occupied for a considerable time the enemy, and facilitated the operations of the Swedes in other quarters. New allies arose to join the Swedes, and it was sufficiently fortunate for them that they compelled Lower Saxony to embrace a neutrality.

Favoured by these important advantages, and reinforced by 14,000 men from Sweden and Livonia, Bannier opened the campaign of the year 1638, with every expectation of success. The Imperialists, who had taken possession of Upper Pomerania and Mecklenburg, either abandoned their posts, or deserted in troops

troops to the Swedish colours, to avoid that hunger which was their most formidable enemy in those exhausted countries; such repeated marching and quarters wasted the territory between the Elbe and the Oder, and Bannier was under the necessity, to avoid having his army starved on its march, of making a circuit from Lower Pomerania through Lower Saxony, and fell into the electorate of Saxony from Halberstadt; the impatience of the Lower Saxon states to rid themselves of such a guest, made them provide him with the necessary provisions, so that his troops had bread at Magdeburg, a country where hunger had already overcome men's disgust at human flesh.

He spread consternation among the Saxons by his approach; but it was not on that exhausted country, but upon the hereditary dominions of Austria, that his designs were bent; the Duke of Weimar's victories encouraged him, and the prosperous state of the Austrian provinces excited his avarice. After he had beaten the Imperial general Salis at Elsterbug, annihilated the Saxon army near Chemnitz, and taken Pirna, he entered Bohemia with irresistible impetuosity, crossed the Elbe, threatened

ened Prague, took Brandeis and Leitmeritz, defeated General Hofkirch with ten regiments, and spread terror and devastation throughout that defenceless kingdom; booty was all that was sought, and what could not be removed was destroyed. In order to convey away the new corn, the ears were cut off from the stalks, and the latter burnt; above a thousand castles, hamlets, and villages were laid in ashes, and a hundred were often seen in flames during one night. From Bohemia he extended his ravages to Silesia, and it was his intention to carry them into Austria and Moravia; to prevent this, General Hatzfeld was recalled from Westphalia, and Piccolomini from the Netherlands: the Archduke Leopold, brother to the Emperor, received the chief command, in order to repair the incapacity of his predecessor Gallas, and restore the Imperial army to its former reputation.

The issue justified these new measures, and the campaign which the Swedes began in 1640, appeared to have taken an unfortunate turn for them; they were successively driven from all their posts in Bohemia, and anxious only to secure their plunder, they hastily retreated to the heights of Meissen. But they were pursued

sued by the enemy through Saxony, and being beaten at Plauen, were obliged to retreat into Thuringia. From the summit of success, they were once more humbled only again to recover their former consideration; Bannier's weak army, on the brink of destruction in its camp at Erfurt, suddenly recovered itself: the Dukes of Lunenburg abandoned the treaty of Prague, and joined him with the troops which they had some time before led against him; Hesse Cassel sent reinforcements, and the Duke of Longueville supported him with the late Duke of Weimar's army. Once more superior in numbers to the Imperialists, Bannier offered them battle at Saalfeld; but their general, Piccolomini, prudently avoided it, and occupied a position too strong to be forced. When the Bavarians at length separated from the Imperialists, and directed their march towards Franconia, Bannier attempted an attack upon this divided corps; but his design was frustrated by the skill of the Bavarian general Mercy, and the near approach of the Imperialists. Both armies now entered the exhausted territory of Hesse, where they formed intrenched camps close to each other, until at length hunger and the severity of the winter compelled them to retire. Piccolomini took up his winter-
quarters

quarters upon the rich banks of the Weser, but finding himself outflanked by Bannier, he was obliged to abandon them and retreat into Franconia.

At this period a diet was held at Ratisbon, where deliberations took place concerning a peace. The presence of the Emperor, who sat as president in the Electoral College, the plurality of voices in favour of the Catholics, the great number of bishops, and the desertion of several Protestant states, inclined the transactions of this assembly to favour the Emperor, and deprived it of every claim to impartiality. The Protestants, not without reason, beheld it as a conspiracy of Austria and its creatures against them, and thought it expedient, as soon as possible, to dissolve such a diet.

Bannier undertook that bold enterprise; his military reputation had already suffered by his retreat out of Bohemia, and required some fresh exploit to recover its former lustre. Without communicating his designs to any person, he left his quarters at Lunenburg in the severest cold of the winter 1641, when the roads and rivers were frozen: accompanied by Marechal de Guebriant, who commanded the French and

and the Duke of Weimar's army, he penetrated through Thuringia and Voigtland, and appeared under the walls of Ratifbon before the diet was apprized of his approach. The confternation of that affembly was inconceivable, and all the deputies immediately prepared themfelves for flight; the Emperor alone declared he would not forfake the town, and encouraged the reft by his example: to the misfortune of the Swedes, a thaw came on, which rendered the Danube impaffable, either by boats or a bridge, by reafon of the large pieces of ice which were carried down the ftream. Perfonally to infult the Emperor, Bannier fired 500 cannon fhots againft the town, which, however, caufed no great mifchief. Difappointed in his fcheme, he now refolved to penetrate into Bavaria and Moravia, which was defencelefs, in order to procure a rich booty, and more comfortable winter-quarters for his troops; but no perfuafions could prevail upon the French general to follow him; Guebriant feared a defign was formed to remove Weimar's army fo far from the Rhine as to be able to gain it over, or prevent its acting independently. He accordingly feparated from Bannier, and returned towards the Maine, by which the Swede faw himfelf expofed to the whole force of of the Imperial army, which secretly assembled between Ratisbon and Ingolstadt, and advanced against him. He was now to begin a retreat in face of an enemy superior in cavalry, between rivers, woods, and hostile territories. He immediately entered the Forest, intending to retire through Bohemia and Saxony; but he was obliged to abandon three of his regiments at Neuburg. These held, during four entire days, the enemy at bay behind an old wall, and gained time for Bannier to escape. He retreated near Egra to Annaberg: Piccolomini pursued him, by a shorter route, through Schlakkenwald, and was only half an hour too late to seize the passes at Prisnitz, and destroy the Swedish army. Guebriant again formed a junction with Bannier's army, and both directed their march to Halberstadt, after having in vain endeavoured to defend the river Sala against the Austrians.

Bannier at length terminated his career at Halberstadt in May 1641, a victim to disappointment and vexation. He maintained with great renown, though with various success, the reputation of the Swedish arms in Germany, and showed himself, by a train of victories, to be worthy of his great master in the art of war.

war. He was fertile in expedients, and formed, with impenetrable secrecy, designs, which he executed with boldness; greater in adversity than in good fortune, and never more formidable than when at the brink of destruction: but his military talents were tarnished with that unamiable disposition which but too often accompanies the soldier. Equally haughty in private life as at the head of his army, boisterous as his profession, and proud as a conqueror, he oppressed the German princes no less by his pride than by his contributions in their territories: after his warlike toils he regaled himself by the joys of the table, which he indulged to excess, and which brought him to an early grave. But though addicted to pleasure as much as Alexander or Mahomet II. he could in a moment forsake it to resume the dangers of his command; near 80,000 men fell in the many battles in which he was engaged, and 600 standards and colours which he took from the enemy and sent to Stockholm, were trophies of his victories. The loss of this celebrated general was immediately felt by the Swedes, and it was feared that such a man could not be replaced; the spirit of insubordination, retained within bounds by the great authority of Bannier, awoke upon his death;

the officers with an alarming unanimity demanded their dismissal, and none of the four generals who shared the command after Bannier could silence these discontents; discipline was at an end; increasing want, and the Imperial citations, daily diminished the forces; the French army showed little zeal; the Lunenburgers forsook the Swedish colours after the Princes of the House of Brunswic, upon the death of Duke George, had formed a treaty with the Emperor; and at length even the Hessians quitted them, in order to seek better quarters in Westphalia. The enemy profited by these calamitous circumstances, and though defeated with loss in two pitched battles, succeeded in making a considerable progress in Lower Saxony.

At length appeared the new Swedish generalissimo with fresh troops and money. This was Torstenson, a pupil of Gustavus Adolphus, and his most successful imitator, who had been his page during the Polish war. Although a martyr to the gout, and labouring under this most severe complaint, he displayed more activity than his enemy: under him the theatre of war was changed, and new maxims were adopted, which necessity required and the

the issue justified. Austria's territories had not yet felt the miseries which raged in the rest of Germany; it was Torstenson who first procured Austria that bitter experience.

In Silesia the enemy had gained considerable advantages over the Swedish general Stalhantsch, and drove him to Neumark; Torstenson, who joined the Swedish army in Lunenburg, called him to his assistance, and in the year 1642, marched through Brandenburg into Silesia, where the former, under the great Elector, began to maintain a neutrality. Glogau was taken by storm, without approaches or a breach; Francis Albert, Duke of Lauenburg, was defeated at Schweidnitz; on this occasion that general was shot through the body, Schweidnitz taken, and all Silesia upon the hither side of the Oder conquered. The Swedes now penetrated into Moravia, where no enemy of Austria had hitherto appeared, took Olmutz, and put even Vienna in consternation.

Meanwhile the Archduke Leopold and Piccolomini had assembled a superior force, which speedily drove the Swedish conquerors from Moravia, and, after a fruitless attempt upon Breig, from all Silesia. Reinforced by Wrangel,

gel, the Swedes turned upon the enemy, and relieved Glogau; but they could neither bring the Imperialists to a battle, nor execute their own designs upon Bohemia. Torstenson now **overrun** Lusatia, where, in presence of the enemy, he took Zittau, and in a short time directed his march towards the Elbe, which he passed at Torgau: he threatened Leipzig with a siege, after that city had, during ten years, experienced none of those miseries with which the war afflicted the rest of Germany.

Leopold and Piccolomini instantly hastened to relieve Leipzig, and Torstenson, to avoid being enclosed between the enemy's army and the town, advanced against the Austrians in order of battle. By an unaccountable fatality, both armies met exactly at the same spot upon which Gustavus Adolphus, eleven years before, had eternized his memory by a decisive victory, and the former intrepidity encouraged the present combatants to equal it by a noble emulation. The Swedish generals Stalhantsch and Willenberg rushed with such impetuosity against the left wing of the Austrians, which had not as yet regularly formed, that their horse was put into confusion, and that division of the Imperial army was separated from the
cavalry

cavalry which covered it, and was routed: but the left of the Swedes was threatened with a similar fate, when the victorious right wing hastened to its assistance, took the enemy in flank and rear, and divided the Austrian lines. The infantry on both sides, after expending their ammunition, engaged in a furious conflict, until the Austrians, at length surrounded upon every side, were, after a contest of three hours, compelled to abandon the field. The generals of both armies did their utmost to rally their flying troops, and the Archduke Leopold was the first who came with his regiments to the attack, as well as the last who fled. This victory cost the Swedes above 3000 men, together with two of their best generals, Schlangen and Lilienhoeck; near 5000 of the Austrians remained dead upon the field, and an equal number were taken prisoners; their entire artillery, consisting of forty-six cannon, the silver plate and archives of the Archduke, fell into the conqueror's hands. Torstenson, disabled too much by his victory to pursue the enemy, advanced to Leipzig; the defeated army retired to Bohemia, where the dispersed regiments reassembled. The Archduke Leopold could not bear this defeat; and a regiment of cavalry, which by its early flight occasioned the disaster,

parti-

particularly felt his indignation; he publicly at Raconitz, in presence of the army, declared it infamous, took away its horses, arms, and insignia, ordered its standards to be torn, condemned to death several of the officers, and decimated the private men.

Leipzig itself, which surrendered three weeks after, was the most brilliant consequence of this victory; the city was obliged to clothe the Swedish army anew, and a tax of 300,000 rix-dollars was imposed upon the foreign merchants who had their warehouses in the city, to redeem them from plunder. Torstenson advanced in the middle of winter against Freyberg, bid defiance to the inclemency of the season for several weeks before that town, and hoped by his perseverance to conquer the resolution of the garrison; but he only fruitlessly sacrificed his men, and the approach of the Imperial general Piccolomini compelled him to abandon his enterprise; he, however, regarded it as an advantage to have disturbed the enemy in their winter-quarters, and made them lose 3000 horses. He now turned towards the Oder, in order to reinforce himself by the garrisons of Silesia and Pomerania; but he suddenly returned to Bohemia, traversed that kingdom, and

and relieved Olmutz, which was threatened by the Imperialists. In his camp at Doditschau, two miles from Olmutz, he commanded all Moravia, raised heavy contributions, and made excursions as far as Vienna; it was in vain that the Emperor armed the nobility of Hungary to defend that province; these claimed their privileges, and refused to quit their native country; time was lost by negotiation, and the entire province was abandoned to the fury of the Swedes.

While Torstenson astonished Europe by his progress, the allied army had not remained inactive in another part of the Empire. The Hessians and the troops of Weimar had fallen into the electorate of Cologn, under Count Erberstein, in order to take up their winterquarters in that bishopric; to rid himself of those troublesome guests, the Elector called to his aid the Imperial general Hatzfeld, and assembled his own troops under General Lamboy. These the allies attacked at Kempen, in January 1642, and totally defeated them in a great battle, wherein 2000 were killed, and double that number taken prisoners. This important victory opened the entrance into the electorate, and the allies were not only able to maintain their winter-quarters there, but to draw from the country great supplies of men and horses.

Guebriant left the Hessians to defend their conquests upon the Lower Rhine against Hatzfeld, and advanced towards Thuringia, with a view to second the progress of Torstenson; but instead of joining the Swedes, he retired to the Maine and Rhine, from which he had too far removed. As the Bavarians under Mercy and John de Werth were arrived before him in the margraviate of Baden, he was under the necessity of wandering for several weeks in the open air, amid all the severity of the season, until he at length took up his winter-quarters in Brisgau after a disastrous expedition. In the ensuing summer he indeed occupied the Bavarian army in Suabia in such a manner that it could not relieve Thionville, which was besieged by the Prince of Condé; he was at length, however, driven into Alsace, where he awaited a reinforcement.

The death of Cardinal Richelieu, which took place in 1642, and the subsequent change of the throne and of ministry, which the death of Louis XIII. occasioned, withdrew the attention

tion of the French for some time from the transactions in Germany, and caused their inactivity in the field. But Mazarine inherited Richelieu's power, his principles, and projects; he followed the plans of his predecessor with redoubled zeal, however the French subjects were to suffer for the political greatness of their nation. If Richelieu employed his principal force against Spain, Mazarine turned it against the Emperor; and the care with which he carried on the war, showed that he considered the German armies as the best shield of France. Immediately after the siege of Thionville he detached a considerable reinforcement to the assistance of Field-marshal Guebriant in Alsace; and in order to inspire his troops with the greater ardour, the famous conqueror at Rocroi, the Duke of Enguien, afterwards Prince of Condé, was placed at their head. Guebriant now felt himself sufficiently strong to appear again with reputation in Germany; he accordingly passed the Rhine with a view of procuring better winter-quarters in Suabia, and actually made himself master of Rothweil, where the Bavarian magazine fell into his hands. But this place cost more than it was worth, and was recovered more speedily than it had been taken; Guebriant received a wound in the arm,

arm, which the unskilfulness of his surgeon rendered mortal; and the greatness of his loss was perceived on the very day of his death.

The French army, visibly diminished by this expedition in a severe season, had, after the capture of Rothweil, withdrawn to the neighbourhood of Duttlingen, where, without expecting an attack, they lay in great security. Meanwhile the enemy assembled a formidable force to prevent the French from approaching near Bavaria, and to save the country from their ravages. The Imperialists under Hatzfeld joined the Bavarians under Mercy; and even the Duke of Lorrain, who, during the whole course of this war, is found every where but in his own dutchy, joined the combined armies with his troops. It was resolved to beat up the French quarters in Duttlingen and the neighbouring villages. This was during the war a very favourite species of expedition, and being commonly accompanied with confusion, cost the lives of more men than a regular battle. The French soldier upon this occasion was unaccustomed to the severity of the German winter, and being totally unprepared

pared for such an undertaking, never thought of a surprise. John de Werth, who was esteemed a master in this species of warfare, and who had been lately exchanged for Gustavus Horn, commanded the attempt, and succeeded, contrary to every expectation.

The attack was made on a side where it was least expected, by reason of the woods and numerous hollow ways; and a violent snow which fell upon the same day (the 24th of November 1643) concealed the approach of the vanguard until it halted before Duttlingen. All the artillery without the place, together with the castle of Hemburg, was taken without resistance; Duttlingen itself was soon after surrounded by the army, and its communication cut off with the adjacent villages. The French were vanquished without firing a cannon: their cavalry owed their safety to a speedy flight; their infantry were either cut in pieces or voluntarily laid down their arms. Near 2000 men were killed, and 7000, together with twenty staff officers and ninety captains, surrendered as prisoners. This was, perhaps, the only victory in the whole war which made an equal impression upon the party which gained

and

and that which loſt*: both were Germans, and it was the French who diſgraced themſelves. The memory of that unfortunate day, which was renewed a hundred years later at Roſsbach, was indeed eraſed by the ſubſequent exploits of a Condé and a Turenne; but the Germans thought they had acquired much, and indemnified themſelves for all the miſeries which French politics brought, by caſting a reflection upon their intrepidity.

This defeat of the French was, however, very pernicious to the Swedes, as the Emperor's army could now act united, and their enemies were conſiderably increaſed. Torſtenſon had ſuddenly abandoned Moravia in September 1643, and retired to Sileſia. The cauſe of this ſtep was a ſecret, and the ſtrange direction of his marches

---

* The victory at Roſsbach excited as much joy among the Auſtrians, as among the Pruſſians who gained it. National pride could not refrain from exultation at the idea of 22,000 Pruſſians ſeeing 60,000 French advance while they were quietly cooking their dinners, and afterwards defeating them. Towards the concluſion of the battle a Pruſſian dragoon had made a French ſoldier priſoner, when he ſaw an Auſtrian cuiraſſier behind him, with his ſword uplifted to cut him down: " Brother German," cried the Pruſſian, " leave me the Frenchman."—" Aye, take him," anſwered the Auſtrian, and galloped away. *Tranſ.*

increased the general perplexity of men. From Silesia, after numberless circuits, he marched towards the Elbe, where the Austrians followed him as far as Lusatia. He laid a bridge over the Elbe at Torgau, and spread a report that he intended to penetrate through Meissen into the Upper Palatinate and Bavaria. He also, at Barby, pretended to pass the river, but meanwhile gradually retreated from the Elbe as far as Havelberg, where he astonished his troops by informing them that he was to lead them against the Danes in Holstein.

Christian IV. King of Denmark had long displayed his jealousy of the Swedes by the obstacles which he placed to the progress of their arms, the vexations which he laid upon their navigation in the Sound, the burdens which he imposed upon their commerce; and, by exceeding all bounds, at length excited their indignation. However dangerous it seemed to engage in a new war while the old was so oppressive, and while the Swedes sunk even under their victories, the desire of revenge and an old antipathy surmounted every consideration, and the embarrassment in which they found themselves was a new incentive to try their fortune against the Danes.

Matters

Matters were at length come to such extremity, that the war was prosecuted only to procure subsistence and labour for the troops, and they only contended for winter-quarters, which were more valued than a decisive victory. But almost all the provinces of Germany were laid waste; they were destitute of provisions, of men, and horses—articles which Holstein possessed in abundance. If the army could even be recruited in this province, and the cavalry newly mounted, the attempt was well repaid. It was of the utmost consequence to check the pernicious influence of Denmark at the commencement of the negotiation, to delay the peace itself, which seemed not to favour Sweden; and when an indemnification came to be debated, to increase its conquests, and endeavour to preserve them. The ill situation of Denmark justified still greater projects, if suddenly executed. In fact, the secret was so well kept in Stockholm, that the Danish minister had not the least suspicion of it; and neither France nor Holland was let into the scheme. The war was instantly commenced without a previous declaration, and Torstenson appeared in Holstein before hostilities were expected. The Swedes instantly overran the dutchy, and made themselves masters of every strong place, Rensburg

burg and Gluckstadt excepted. Another army broke into Schonen, which surrendered without resistance, and it was only the severity of the season which prevented the enemy from crossing the Lesser Baltic, and carrying the war into Fuhnen and Zealand. The Danish fleet was unsuccessful at Femern, and the King himself, who was on board, lost his right eye by a splinter. Cut off from all communication with his distant ally the Emperor, this king was on the point of seeing his dominions overrun by the Swedes, and of fulfilling an old prophecy attributed to the famous Tycho Brahe, viz. That Christian IV. should, in the year 1643, wander in great misery from his dominions.

But the Emperor could not behold with indifference the Danes become subject to Sweden. Notwithstanding the difficulties attending so long a march through desolated provinces, he sent his general, Gallas, who, after Piccolomini's resignation, obtained the supreme command anew, with an army into Holstein. Gallas accordingly appeared in that duchy, took Kiel, and hoped, after his junction with the Danes, to shut up the Swedish army in Jutland. At the same time the Hessians and
the

the Swedish general Koenigsmark were occupied by Hatzfeld and the Bishop of Bremen, son of Christian IV. The latter was obliged to go to Saxony, by reason of an attack upon Meissen: but Torstenson penetrated through the pass between Schleswig and Stapelholm, advanced with his augmented army against Gallas, whom he drove along the Elbe as far as Bernburg, where the Imperialists intrenched themselves. Torstenson passed the Sala, and took such a position in rear of the enemy as cut off their communications with Saxony and Bohemia. Hunger now began to destroy them in great multitudes; nor did their retreat to Magdeburg remedy their desperate situation. The cavalry, which endeavoured to effect its escape to Silesia, was overtaken and totally dispersed at Interbock, while the rest of the army, after a vain attempt to fight its way through the Swedes, was almost wholly destroyed near Magdeburg. A few thousand men, and the reputation of being a consummate master in the art of ruining an army, was all that Gallas brought back of his great force. After this unfortunate attempt to relieve him, the King of Denmark sued for a peace, which he accordingly obtained at Bremseboor, in the year 1645, under very hard conditions.

Torstenson

Torstenson closely pursued his victory. While his inferior generals Lilienstern threatened Saxony, and Koenigsmark subdued all Bremen, he, at the head of 16,000 men and eighty pieces of cannon, broke into Bohemia, and once more endeavoured to remove the seat of war into the hereditary dominions of Austria. Ferdinand, upon receiving intelligence of this, repaired in person to Prague, in order, by his presence, to encourage his subjects; and as a skilful general was so much wanted, and so little harmony reigned among the numerous commanders, he could the more easily assist their operations by being so near the scene. In consequence of his orders Hatzfeld assembled the whole force of Austria and Bavaria, and, contrary to his opinion and desire, formed the Emperor's last army in order of battle, opposite the approaching enemy at Iankowitz, on the 24th of February 1645. Ferdinand depended upon his cavalry, which was 3000 stronger than that of the Swedes, and still more upon the promise of the Virgin Mary, who had appeared to him in a dream, and given the strongest assurances of a complete victory.

Torstenson, who never considered the number of his enemy, was by no means intimidated by their superiority. On the first attack, the left wing, which the general of the League, Goetz, had entangled in a very disadvantageous situation among dikes and thickets, was totally routed, the general himself with the greater part of his men killed, and almost all the ammunition of the army taken. This unfortunate commencement decided the fate of the day. The Swedes, continually advancing, gained some important heights, and at the end of a bloody contest which lasted eight hours, after a vigorous attack of the Imperial cavalry, and a brave resistance of the infantry, they remained masters of the field. Two thousand Austrians were killed upon the spot, and Hatzfeld with 3000 of his men were taken prisoners. Thus did the Emperor in one day lose his best general and his last army.

This victory at Iankowitz at once exposed to the enemy all the states of Austria. Ferdinand hastily fled to Vienna, in order to provide for its safety, and save his family and his treasure. In a short time the Swedes broke into Moravia and Austria with great impetuosity. After they had conquered almost all Moravia, invested

vested Brinn, and possessed themselves of every strong hold as far as the Danube, and at length taken the intrenchments at the Wolf's Bridge near Vienna, they appeared before that capital; and the care which they took to fortify their conquests promised no short visit. After a long and destructive circuit through the different provinces of the German Empire, the war at length returned to where it commenced, and the thunder of the Swedish artillery reminded the inhabitants of Vienna of those balls which twenty-seven years before the Bohemian rebels fired against the Imperial residence. Former scenes were also renewed. Bethlen Gabor's successor, Ragotzy, was invited by Torstenson to his aid, as his predecessor had been by the rebellious Bohemians. He immediately overran Upper Hungary with his troops, and his junction with the Swedes was daily apprehended. The Elector of Saxony, driven to necessity by the Swedes taking up their quarters in his territories, and abandoned by the Emperor, who, after the defeat at Iankowitz, was unable to defend himself, at length embraced the only expedient which remained, and concluded with the Swedes a cessation of hostilities which was renewable every year. The Emperor thus lost an ally while an enemy entered his territories,

territories, his armies were going to decay, and his confederates were defeated in the other extremity of Germany. The French had effaced the shame of their defeat at Duttlingen by a brilliant campaign, and occupied the whole force of Bavaria on the Rhine and in Suabia. Reinforced by troops from France, which Turenne, who had already gained renown by his victories in Italy, brought to the Duke of Enguien, the French appeared before Freyburg on the 3d of August 1644; that town having been shortly before taken by Mercy, and covered by him with his whole army strongly intrenched. But all the impetuosity of the French failed against the firmness of the Bavarians; and the Duke of Enguien was at length compelled to retire, after an useless sacrifice of 6000 of his men. Mazarine shed tears on hearing this great loss, which the heart of Condé, callous to every passion but that of glory, little valued: *The strumpets of Paris*, he was heard to say, *will supply the loss in one night*. Nevertheless the Bavarians were so exhausted by this murderous battle, that they were not in a condition to relieve Austria, nor even defend the banks of the Rhine. Spires, Worms, and Manheim surrendered; and the strong fortress of Philipsburg was taken by famine. Even Mentz

Mentz hastened by a timely surrender to disarm the conquerors.

Austria and Moravia were saved from Torstenson as they had already been from the Bohemians. Ragotzy had advanced at the head of 25,000 of his troops, near the Swedish camp; but these wild undisciplined hordes only ravaged the country, and caused a great want of provisions in the army, instead of assisting Torstenson by any vigorous enterprise. To render the Emperor anxious for his revenues, and the subjects for their property, was Ragotzy's design, as it had been that of Bethlen Gabor; and each returned home after obtaining his ends. Ferdinand granted the barbarian whatever conditions he demanded, and saved himself, by a small sacrifice of territory, from the indignation of that formidable enemy.

The principal force of the Swedes had, in the mean time, greatly exhausted itself in a tedious encampment before Brinn. Torstenson, who commanded, exhausted, during four entire months, his whole system of attack. The defence equalled the attack, and despair augmented the resolution of the Governor de Souches,

Souches, a Swedish deserter who expected no mercy. The ravages which were made by sickness, want, and hardship, the usual consequences of a tedious encampment, together with the departure of the Transylvanians, at length compelled the Swedish general to raise the siege. All the passes towards the Danube were occupied, but, as his army was diminished by hunger and sickness, he relinquished his plan of operations against Austria and Moravia, and contented himself with leaving garrisons in the strong places he had taken, in order to maintain the entry into both those provinces, and marched towards Bohemia, where he was followed by the Imperialists under the Archduke Leopold. Such places as he had not recovered were taken after his departure by the Austrian general Bucheim, so that the following year the frontiers of Austria were fully delivered from the enemy, and Vienna, which trembled for its safety, was relieved from its consternation. Even in Bohemia and Silesia the Swedes only maintained themselves with various success, and traversed both countries without being able to preserve a footing in them. But if Torstenson's designs were not accompanied with all the success which they promised in the commencement, they had the most important con-

consequences for the Swedish party. Denmark was compelled to a peace, Saxony to a neutrality; the Emperor was brought to greater concessions, France became more complaisant, and the behaviour of Sweden towards both these powers was more bold and circumspect. Having performed his duty in the most brilliant manner, the general, crowned with laurels, returned to the station of a private man, and fought by retirement to recover his health.

The Emperor, after Torstenson's retreat, saw himself secured from an irruption into Bohemia; but a new danger soon approached from Suabia and Bavaria. Turenne, who had divided his force from Condé, was, in 1645, near Mergentheim, totally defeated by Mercy, and the victorious Bavarians entered Hesse Cassel under their intrepid leader. But Condé hastened with considerable succours from Alsace, Koenigsmark from Moravia, and the Hessians from the Rhine, to recruit the defeated army, and the Bavarians were in their turn compelled to retreat to the extremity of Suabia. They posted themselves at Allersheim, near Nordlingen, in order to cover the confines of Bavaria; but the impetuosity of Condé was checked by no obstacle; he led on his troops against the enemy's intrenchments, and a bloody battle ensued, which the heroic resistance of the Bavarians rendered the most obstinate and murderous, and at length, by the death of the great Mercy *, the courage of Turenne, and the firmness of the Hessians, terminated in favour of the allies. But this second barbarous sacrifice of men had little effect either upon the progress of the war or the negotiations for peace; the French army, diminished by such an obstinate battle, was still more so by the departure of the Hessians; and the Archduke Leopold brought so many Imperial reinforcements to the Bavarians, that Turenne was immediately obliged to retire over the Rhine.

* This was the man upon whose tomb the beautiful motto, so much celebrated by Voltaire and other modern writers, was engraved:

   Siste viator, heroem calcas!
   Stop, traveller, you tread on a hero!

He was one of the most illustrious of modern generals; nothing could be a greater proof of it than his beating the celebrated Turenne. Had he not, while giving his orders from a steeple in the village which was set on fire, been unfortunately killed by a random shot, he would, upon this occasion, have certainly maintained the field of battle. Condé was wounded in the arm, and the Bavarians made a brilliant retreat with seventy colours they had taken from the enemy. Turenne and Condé had the respect to visit the place of his interment. *Transf.*

The retreat of the French now enabled the enemy to turn his entire force againſt the Swedes in Bohemia. Wrangel, a worthy ſucceſſor of Baunier and Torſtenſon, had obtained the chief command of the Swediſh army in 1646, which, beſides Koenigſmark's flying corps, and the different garriſons diſperſed through the Empire, amounted to 8000 horſe and 15,000 foot. After the Archduke Leopold had reinforced his army of 24,000 men with twelve regiments of Bavarian cavalry and eighteen of infantry, he advanced againſt Wrangel, and expected to overpower him with his ſuperior force before Koenigſmark could join him, or the French make a diverſion. But the Swede did not await him, and he haſtened through Upper Saxony to the Weſer, where he took Hoexter and Paderborn: from thence he marched to Heſſe Caſſel, in order to join Turenne, and in his camp at Wetzlar was joined by the flying corps of Koenigſmark. But Turenne, reſtrained by the inſtructions of Mazarine, who became jealous of the martial prowefs and increaſing power of the Swedes, excuſed himſelf from the preſſing neceſſity of defending the frontiers of France towards the Netherlands, ſince the Dutch did not make the diverſion they had promiſed. But as Wrangel

perſiſted

persisted in his just demands, and as a further refusal would have excited a distrust on the part of the Swedes, and perhaps have led them to conclude a private treaty with the Emperor, Turenne at length received the desired orders to join the Swedish army.

The junction took place at Gieffen, and they now felt themselves in sufficient strength to oppose the enemy. The latter had followed the Swedes to Hesse, where they endeavoured to intercept the convoys, and to prevent their junction with Turenne; both these designs failed, and the Imperialists now saw themselves cut off from the Maine, and reduced to great distress by the loss of their magazines. Wrangel took advantage of their distress, in order to execute a plan which was intended to give the war another turn; he had also adopted the maxim of his predecessors, to carry the war into the Austrian territories; but discouraged by the ill success of Torstenson's enterprise, he expected to attain his ends by a safer method. He accordingly determined to follow the course of the Danube, and to advance against the frontiers of Austria from the centre of Bavaria: a similar plan had formerly been laid by Gustavus Adolphus, but which could not

not be executed, having been suddenly called away from his victorious progress by Wallenstein's army, and the danger which threatened Saxony. His footsteps were pursued by the Duke of Weimar, who, more fortunate than Gustavus Adolphus, had carried his victorious arms between the Iser and the Inn; but he was also compelled to retire by the approach of his numerous enemies. Wrangel now hoped to be able to accomplish this object, **as the Imperial-Bavarian armies were far in his rear on the river Lahn, and could only arrive in Bavaria by a very long march through Franconia and the Upper Palatinate:** he suddenly marched towards the Danube, defeated a body of Bavarians near Donauwerth, and passed that river, as also the Lech, without opposition; but by fruitlessly laying siege to Augsburg, he gained time for the Imperialists not only **to relieve that city, but even to repulse him as far as Lauingen**. But while, in order to remove the seat of war from Bavaria, the enemy turned towards Suabia, he took the opportunity to repass the Lech, which was defenceless, and maintained it against the Imperialists. Bavaria now lay exposed; French and Swedes immediately overran it, and indemnified themselves for all their past dangers by the most cruel

ravages;

ravages; the arrival of the Imperial-Bavarian armies, which at length paſſed the Lech at Thierhaupten, only augmented the miseries of a country which was indiscriminately plundered by friends and enemies.

It was now, for the firſt time, that the firmneſs of Maximilian began to abate, after having, during twenty-eight years, braved every calamity. Ferdinand II. his ſchool-fellow at Ingolſtadt, and the companion of his youth, was no more; and with the death of that friend and benefactor, his attachment was in a great meaſure withdrawn from Auſtria. Private friendſhip and gratitude had attached him to the father; ſtate intereſt alone could connect him with the ſon, to whom he was a ſtranger.

It was by political conſiderations that French duplicity now ſought to detach him from the alliance of Auſtria, and prevailed upon him to lay down his arms. It was not without a great deſign that Mazarine concealed his jealouſy of the increaſing power of the Swedes, and permitted the French to accompany them to Bavaria. That country was deſtined to experience all the miſeries of war, in order to overcome the Elector's firmneſs, and to deprive the Emperor

peror of his most powerful ally. Brandenburg had, under its great Elector, embraced a neutrality; Saxony was compelled to the same step; the Spaniards were forced, by a war with France, to relinquish every share in that of Germany; Denmark had concluded a peace, and Poland prolonged its cessation of hostilities. If the Elector of Bavaria could be detached from the alliance of Austria, the Emperor was exposed to inevitable destruction.

Ferdinand III. saw his danger, and left no means untried to avert the storm; but the Elector had been persuaded that the Spaniards alone prevailed upon the Emperor to oppose the peace. Maximilian hated the Spaniards mortally, because they had resisted his attempt to procure the Palatinate; it was by no means his intention to expose himself to ruin for so ungrateful a power, and he thought he should sufficiently fulfil his duty to the Emperor by embracing a neutral system.

The deputies of the three crowns, and of Bavaria, assembled at Ulm, in order to conclude a cessation of hostilities. The instructions of the Austrian ambassador, however, soon showed that it was not the Emperor's intention

intention to bring the congress to a pacific conclusion: the Swedes, who had every thing to hope from a continuance of the war, were not inclined to bear unfavourable conditions; they were conquerors, and still the Emperor seemed disposed to dictate to them. In the first transports of indignation, their deputies would have left the congress if the French had not had recourse to threats.

After the Elector of Bavaria's good intentions had failed to conclude a peace for the Emperor, he thought it time to provide for himself; whatever might be his sacrifices, he considered it his duty to abandon the war. He agreed that the Swedes should extend their quarters in Suabia and Franconia, and confined his own to Bavaria and the Palatinate; his conquests in Suabia were exchanged for those which the Swedes had made in Bavaria: Cologn and Hesse Cassel were also included in this cessation of hostilities. After the conclusion of this treaty, upon the 14th of March 1647, the French and Swedes retired to separate winter-quarters, the former in the dutchy of Wirtemberg, and the latter in Upper Suabia, near the lake of Bode. At the northern extremity of that lake, and the southern frontier of Suabia,

bia, the Austrian town of Bregentz defied every attack by its steep and narrow passes; and the neighbouring people had, with their property, taken refuge in it from all quarters for security. The probability of a rich booty, and the advantage of obtaining a pass into Tirol, Switzerland, and Italy, determined the Swedish general to venture an attack upon this important place; he succeeded, although six thousand peasants attempted to defend the pass against him. In the mean time Turenne had, according to agreement, marched towards Wirtemberg, where he forced the Landgrave of Darmstadt and the Elector of Mentz to embrace a neutrality after the example of Bavaria.

French policy now seemed to have obtained its ends in withdrawing from the Emperor all his allies, and compelling him to a peace. That once so powerful prince had only an army of 12,000 men remaining; and as he had lost his best generals, he was compelled to intrust the command of these to a Calvinist, Melander, a deserter from the Hessians. But by a fortune peculiar to this war, the events of which often deceived the calculations of policy, the apparently ruined force of Austria reassumed a dangerous superiority. The jealousy of France towards the

the Swedes did not permit it to suffer the latter entirely to ruin the Emperor and obtain a footing in the German Empire, which might prove fatal to the French themselves; no advantage was therefore taken of the diftress of Auftria; and Turenne's army, feparating from that of Wrangel, marched to the borders of the Netherlands. Wrangel endeavoured, after he had entered Franconia, where he took Schweinfurt, and enrolled its Imperial garrifon among his troops, to penetrate into Bohemia, and had laid fiege to Egra, the key to that kingdom. To relieve that town, the Emperor in perfon advanced with his laft army; but being obliged to make a confiderable circuit, in order to fpare the eftates of the prefident of the council of war, the march was prolonged, and before he arrived, Egra was already taken. Both armies approached fo clofe to each other, that a decifive battle was expected, especially as the Imperialifts were the more numerous; but the latter contented themfelves with haraffing the Swedes by hunger, fkirmifhes, and fatiguing marches, until the Emperor had attained his wifhes by the negotiations which he opened with Bavaria.

The neutrality of Bavaria inflicted a wound which the Court of Vienna could never pardon, and which, after fruitless endeavours to prevent, it resolved, if possible, to turn to advantage. A multitude of Bavarian officers were upon this occasion deprived of employment, and consequently absolved from their allegiance; even the brave General de Werth was among the discontented, and formed a plot to deliver the Bavarian army to the Emperor, who encouraged him to that step. Ferdinand was not ashamed to favour this piece of treachery against his father's most faithful ally; he formally issued a proclamation recalling the Bavarian troops from their allegiance, and reminding them that they belonged to the Empire, and were only raised by the Elector by Imperial authority. Fortunately for Maximilian, he discovered the conspiracy in sufficient time to be able, by the most vigorous efforts, to impede its execution.

Such faithless conduct might have justified reprisals; but Maximilian was too old a statesman to listen to the voice of passion where policy alone was concerned. He had not procured by the truce the advantages which he expected; so far from accelerating a peace, his neutrality had a pernicious influence upon

upon the negotiations at Munſter and Oſnaburg, where the allied powers increaſed their demands, conſcious of their ſuperiority. The French and Swedes were removed from Bavaria; but by loſing his quarters in Suabia, he ſaw himſelf obliged to maintain his troops at home, if he did not altogether diſband them, and expoſe his dominions at ſuch a critical conjuncture to every invader. Before he embraced either of thoſe dangerous alternatives, he reſolved to break the neutrality, and once more take up arms.

This reſolution, and the immediate ſuccour which he ſent the Emperor, compelled Wrangel to evacuate Bohemia. He retired through Thuringia towards Weſtphalia and Lunenburg, in order to join the French forces under Turenne, and was followed by the Imperial-Bavarian army under Melander and Gronsfeld as far as the Weſer. His ruin was inevitable if overtaken by the enemy before he had formed a junction with Turenne; but the Swedes were ſaved upon this occaſion as the Emperor had formerly been; the Court liſtened to the maxims of ſound policy according as it beheld the approach of peace; the Elector of Bavaria could not ſafely appear to contribute ſo much

to

to the superiority of the Emperor, and this circumstance hastened the peace. A change of fortune might delay the treaty for several years, and perhaps postpone the tranquillity of all Europe; if France retained Sweden within bounds, the Elector of Bavaria followed that example towards the Emperor, and by prudently withholding his assistance, remained master of the fate of Austria. The power of the Emperor threatened at once to obtain a dangerous superiority, when Maximilian suddenly refused to pursue the Swedes; he also feared the reprisals of France, which threatened to send all Turenne's army against him if he attempted to pass the Weser.

Melander, prevented by the Bavarians from pursuing Wrangel further, marched through Jena and Erfurt against Hesse Cassel, and now appeared as a dangerous enemy in a country which he had once defended. If it was vengeance which excited him to render that country the scene of devastation, he indulged his passion to the utmost. The miseries of that unhappy country became excessive. But the ravager had soon occasion to repent of his substituting revenge for prudence; his army diminished in the exhausted country of Hesse, while

Wrangel

Wrangel collected fresh forces in Lunenburg, and new mounted his cavalry. Too weak to maintain his quarters when the Swedish general opened the campaign in the winter of 1648, and advanced towards Caffel, he was constrained with disgrace to retire, and seek safety upon the banks of the Danube.

France had once more deceived the Swedes; and Turenne's army, notwithstanding Wrangel's remonstrances, retired towards the Rhine: the Swedish general resented this by ordering the cavalry of Weimar to join him, who had left the French service, and by that step increased the jealousy of France. At length Turenne obtained permission to join the Swedes, and the united armies opened the last campaign of this war. They pursued Melander to the Danube, threw supplies into Egra, which was then besieged by the Imperialists, and beat the Imperial-Bavarian army upon the side of the Danube at Sufmarshausen. Melander in this action was mortally wounded, and Gronsfeld posted himself upon the other side of the Lech, in order to prevent the enemy's entrance into Bavaria.

But

But Gronsfeld was not more fortunate than Tilly, who had sacrificed his life in this same post for the preservation of Bavaria. Wrangel and Turenne chose the same spot for passing the river which was distinguished by the victory of Gustavus Adolphus, and succeeded by the advantages which had favoured the latter; Bavaria was once more overrun, and the breach of the treaty punished by the utmost severity towards the Bavarians. Maximilian took refuge in Saltzburg, while the Swedes passed the Iser as far as the Inn; a violent rain, which in a few days swelled this otherwise inconsiderable river to an uncommon height, once more saved Austria from the impending danger; the enemy attempted ten different times to lay a bridge of boats over the Inn, and as often failed. Never were the Catholics in such consternation as upon the present occasion, when the enemy was in the centre of Bavaria, and they no longer possessed a general who could be compared to a Turenne, a Wrangel, or a Koenigsmark. At length the brave Piccolomini arrived from the Netherlands to assume the command of the feeble remains of the Imperialists; the ravages which the allies committed in Bavaria had rendered it impossible for them to subsist longer in that country, and obliged them to retire

retire to the Upper Palatinate, where the intelligence of peace put an end to their future operations.

Koenigfmark advanced with a flying corps towards Bohemia, where Erneft Odovalfky, a captain of cavalry, who had refigned after having been difabled in the Imperial fervice without receiving any penfion, laid before him a plan to furprife the fmaller part of Prague. Koenigfmark fuccceded in this attempt, and thereby obtained the honour of having clofed the thirty years war by the laft memorable action. This decifive blow, which at length overcame the Emperor's irrefolution, only coft the Swedes one man; the old town, the greater half of which is divided by the river Moldaw from the new, occupied by its refiftance the Count Palatine Charles Guftavus, the fucceffor of Chriftina to the throne, who had arrived with frefh troops from Sweden when the entire Swedifh army in Bohemia and Silefia appeared before its walls. The approach of winter at length compelled the befiegers to go into quarters, where they received intelligence that the peace was figned on the 24th of October at Munfter and Ofnaburg.

The

The coloſſal labour of concluding this famous, ever memorable, and holy treaty, which had to combat with the greateſt apparent obſtacles, which was to unite the moſt oppoſite intereſts; the concatenation of circumſtances which muſt have combined to terminate this painful and laborious effort of policy; what it coſt to open the negotiations amid the alternate viciſſitudes of a bloody war, and conclude them under every diſadvantage; what the conditions were of a peace which terminated a bloody war of thirty years, and the influence which it had upon the general ſyſtem of European policy: theſe muſt be left to another pen and a more convenient opportunity. The limits are already ſurpaſſed which the author of the preſent ſketch had originally propoſed; and however great the undertaking was to relate the hiſtory of the war, that of the peace of Weſtphalia is one of no leſs importance. The abridgment of ſuch an event could not here be given with the neceſſary brevity, without reducing to a ſkeleton the moſt intereſting and characteriſtic monument of human wiſdom and paſſions, and thereby depriving it of the attention of the public for which I write, and of which I now reſpectfully take my leave.

APPENDIX.

IT is much to be regretted that the author has left his history incomplete, and did not describe those memorable negotiations which terminated in the most famous of all modern treaties of peace. A subject of such importance, treated by such a master, must be of infinitely more use than the most elaborate descriptions of battles and sieges, which in all ages and circumstances betray a sameness, notwithstanding their apparent effect upon the transactions of men.

Some account of the principal characters mentioned in this ever-memorable war has been added, and it is hoped will not be wholly unacceptable.

AMELIA

AMELIA ELIZABETH, LANDGRAVINE OF HESSE CASSEL.

SHE was the daughter of Philip Louis, Count of Hanau, and espoused the Landgrave of Cassel, to whom she was an example of conjugal affection, besides possessing every beauty of person and accomplishment of mind which could adorn the female sex.

At the age of seventeen she married a prince of merit, by whom she had fifteen children. While her husband was engaged in the general war, she took every care to educate her children, and rendered her son William an excellent prince. On the death of her husband, who was reported to have been poisoned, she assumed the administration, in consequence of his will. Though her country, upon the death of the Landgrave, was threatened with destruction, not only by the Austrians but also by the claims of the Landgrave of Darmstadt, she saved it by her prudence until her possessions were secured by the Westphalian peace. In the year 1650 she yielded the sovereignty to her son, and dedicated the remainder of her days

days to peace and meditation. She died in the year 1651.

Few females have accompanied so much beauty and so many accomplishments with such rare abilities and virtues; nor did she ever betray the weakness of a woman, notwithstanding the imminent danger which so frequently terrified the princes of the Empire, and with which she, in the course of this war, was so dangerously threatened.

BERNARD DUKE OF WEIMAR.

THIS celebrated hero was the youngest of nine sons of John Duke of Weimar, and Dorothy Maria, Princess of Anhalt. He possessed an hereditary hatred towards Austria, as being directly descended from the Elector of Saxony who was deprived of his electoral dignity and the greater part of his states by Charles V. (See Robertson's History.)

United in the closest friendship with Gustavus Adolphus, he showed himself not inferior to that consummate general; and when the latter

latter had fallen at Lutzen he assumed the command: by manœuvres which displayed equal skill and intrepidity he obtained, over one of the most celebrated generals which Austria ever produced, a complete victory.

He died suddenly, not without suspicions of poison, when he was about espousing the Landgravine Amelia of Hesse Cassel. He united with his military talents extreme humanity; and, notwithstanding his youth, displayed all the prudence of age. His genius seemed altogether to aspire at something vast and unbounded. If he resembles any character in ancient history, it is Quintus Sertorius.

CHRISTINA QUEEN OF SWEDEN.

THAT princess was only six years old when her father fell at Lutzen. The administration of affairs, which, till her nineteenth year, had been managed by the Chancellor Oxenstern, she assumed in 1645. After having, in the commencement, applied herself with great zeal to state affairs, she afterwards neglected them, and

and wholly devoted herself to literature, having invited a number of learned men to her court, among the rest the celebrated Des Cartes. Her negligence occasioned much disadvantage to her subjects at the peace of Westphalia. The Swedes became discontented with her expending a large portion of her revenues in purchasing the rarities of foreign countries, while she neglected her more important concerns. In order to remedy this, the states desired she would marry; which she refused: and in the year 1651 formally declared she would abdicate the throne, which she actually did in the year 1654. She then went to Italy and France, where she abjured the Protestant faith; and in the latter country was guilty of the atrocious crime of murdering Mondaleschi, a gentleman of her suite who had revealed some of her amours, to which it appears she was much addicted. It was fortunate for her, as Voltaire justly observes, **that** England was not the scene of this inhuman transaction. She afterwards made vain attempts to reascend the throne of Sweden, and died in the year 1689.

OXENSTERN.

THIS extraordinary man has been univerſally regarded as one of the greateſt ſtateſmen of modern times; and is one of thoſe who ſeldom have attained to the height of fortune, and of poſſeſſing throughout Europe an influence of which the greateſt ſovereigns can rarely boaſt. He was an admirer of literature; and it is aſſerted that the ſecond part of the Hiſtory of the Swediſh War in Germany, attributed to Bogiſlaus Philip of Chemnitz, is of his compoſition. He ſucceſsfully employed political writers in his ſtate affairs.

The character of this extraordinary man has been drawn by the Queen of Sweden, Chriſtina, in one of her manuſcripts.

" That great man," ſays ſhe, " had the
" cleareſt underſtanding—the fruit of youthful
" induſtry. In the midſt of his multifarious
" affairs he read much. His penetration was
" quick, and his knowledge of ſtate matters
" was well grounded. He was acquainted
" with the ſtrength and weakneſs of all the
                                    " powers

"　powers of Europe. He united with great
"　experience an extensive genius and a great
"　soul. His activity was indefatigable. Busi-
"　ness was the amusement even of his vacant
"　hours. He was temperate, as far as can be
"　applauded in an age and nation when this
"　was not yet become a virtue. He could be
"　tranquil notwithstanding his extensive occu-
"　pations. He affirmed that he spent only
"　two sleepless nights in his life: the one upon
"　the death of Gustavus Adolphus, and the
"　other at the defeat at Nordlingen. He al-
"　ways laid aside his cares when he undressed
"　himself. He was at the same time ambitious
"　but disinterested: and the features of his
"　character were only disfigured by too great
"　a slowness and phlegm."

THE END.

Printed by S. GOSNELL,
Little Queen Street, Holborn.

www.ingramcontent.com/pod-product-compliance
Lightning Source LLC
Chambersburg PA
CBHW032358230426
43672CB00007B/736